SCOTNOTES
Number 39

Walter Scott's
The Bride of Lammermoor

Eileen Dunlop

Association for Scottish Literary Studies 2018

Published by
Association for Scottish Literary Studies
Scottish Literature
7 University Gardens
University of Glasgow
Glasgow G12 8QH
www.asls.org.uk

ASLS is a registered charity no. SC006535

First published 2019

Text © Eileen Dunlop

All rights reserved. No part of this book may be reproduced, stored in a retrieval system, or transmitted in any form or means, electronic, mechanical, photocopying, recording or otherwise, without the prior permission of the Association for Scottish Literary Studies.

A CIP catalogue for this title
is available from the British Library

ISBN 978-1-906841-38-6

CONTENTS

		Page
1.	The Life of Walter Scott	1
2.	Scott's Poetry and Prose	2
3.	*The Bride of Lammermoor*: A Gothic Novel?	10
4.	Time, Place and the Supernatural	14
5.	Structure and Language	20
6.	The Framing Narrative: Characters and Theme	25
7.	Summary of Chapters 2–35	28
8.	Characters in *The Bride of Lammermoor*	62
9.	Conclusion	77
10.	Further Reading	79

SCOTNOTES

Study guides to major Scottish writers and literary texts

Produced by the Education Committee
of the Association for Scottish Literary Studies

Series Editors
Lorna Borrowman Smith
Ronald Renton

Editorial Board
Ronald Renton
(Convener, Education Committee, ASLS)
Craig Aitchison
Diane Anderson
Gillin Anderson
Laurence Cavanagh
Professor John Corbett
Dr Emma Dymock
Dr Maureen Farrell
Dr Morna Fleming
Dr Simon Hall
Jean Hillhouse
John Hodgart
Bob Hume
Katrina Lucas
Ann MacKinnon
Professor Alan Riach
Dr Gillian Sargent
Dr Cheryl Simpson
Lorna Borrowman Smith

THE ASSOCIATION FOR SCOTTISH LITERARY STUDIES aims to promote the study, teaching and writing of Scottish literature, and to further the study of the languages of Scotland.

To these ends, the ASLS publishes works of Scottish literature; literary criticism and in-depth reviews of Scottish books in *Scottish Literary Review*; and scholarly studies of language in *Scottish Language*. It also publishes *New Writing Scotland*, an annual anthology of new poetry, drama and short fiction, in Scots, English and Gaelic. All these publications are available as a single 'package', in return for an annual subscription.

ASLS also produces a range of teaching materials covering Scottish language and literature for use in schools.

Enquiries should be sent to:

>ASLS
>Scottish Literature
>7 University Gardens
>University of Glasgow
>Glasgow G12 8QH
>
>Tel/fax +44 (0)141 330 5309
>e-mail **office@asls.org.uk**
>or visit our website at **www.asls.org.uk**

A note on the text
Page references are to the Oxford World's Classics edition (1991, reissued 2008), edited by Fiona Robertson.

1. THE LIFE OF WALTER SCOTT

Walter Scott was born on 15 August 1771 in Edinburgh, then a small, crowded town of wynds and closes straggling away from the main High Street. Rich and poor lived in multi-storeyed tenements, teetering above a midge-infested swamp. Despite its past as a royal capital and its present high reputation as a centre of learning, medicine and law, Scott's birthplace was notoriously squalid. Infectious disease was rife and it is unsurprising that Scott (who did not become 'Sir Walter' until he was forty-seven) was a sickly baby, or that six children had died before his two elder brothers were born. Their parents were Walter Scott, a solicitor with the rank of 'Writer to the Signet' and Anne Rutherford, daughter of an eminent professor of medicine at Edinburgh University.

Aged three, the younger Walter Scott suffered an illness then unidentified, but now recognised as poliomyelitis or 'polio', which left him with a paralysed left leg. On Professor Rutherford's advice, he was sent to recuperate at Sandyknowe, near Kelso in the Scottish Borders, the farm of his paternal grandfather. His general health improved, outdoor exercise strengthened his muscles and he learned to walk on his toes. Apart from short periods back in Edinburgh, and at Bath and Prestonpans in vain pursuit of a complete cure, Sandyknowe was his home until he was seven.

During his early years Scott had no formal education. He was slow in learning to read, but there was a rich oral tradition of storytelling in the Borders, and Scott heard from his grandparents of the exploits of his ancestors and their connections to titled families in the area, notably the Dukes of Buccleuch. He was thrilled by tales of their service to the Crown in the fourteenth-century Scottish Wars of Independence, and more recently the Jacobite Risings of 1715 and 1745–46. He also heard recitations of the Border ballads, tales of warlike courage and supernatural happenings. The oral culture of the Border region, along with its haunting landscape, provided a major influence on his mature work.

In 1777, when it was clear that his lameness was incurable, Scott returned to Edinburgh. In his absence, his family had moved to George Square, a new housing development south of the Old Town – the city's first attempt to solve its overcrowding problem. Although he would spend holidays in and around Kelso, Scott now became a city boy.

After intensive tutoring to teach him the basics of Latin and Mathematics, Scott was enrolled at the High School of Edinburgh, an academically well-regarded boys' school, also infamous for its ferocious corporal punishment and unruly pupil behaviour. Realising he was likely to be bullied, Scott set about establishing himself as 'one of the boys', forcing himself to join in rough playground games, violent street fights and dangerous rock-climbing. This 'tough guy' image became a protective device, used through his life to disguise the sensitive, emotional aspects of his personality.

After inadequate preparation, Scott's classroom performance was rarely above average, and the most important part of his education happened outside school. His middle-class father was able to pay for tutoring in modern languages, history and geography. His mother encouraged him to read Shakespeare's plays, Edmund Spenser's *Faerie Queene* and the high-flown epics of the Italian poet Ludovico Ariosto. These books fed his admiration of aristocracy and, importantly, influenced his perception of how 'ladies and gentlemen' should behave.

In 1783, aged only twelve, Scott moved from school to Edinburgh University. His results remained unremarkable and, like most of his fellow-students, he behaved badly – so badly that in 1786 his exasperated father removed him and made him an apprentice in the family business. Scott became an office clerk, copying legal documents by day and spending his wages on books, fishing trips and hanging out with his posh friends at weekends. Deputising for his father, he visited the Highlands for the first time and parts of southern Scotland previously unknown to him.

In 1788, a craze for German literature hit Edinburgh; death-laden ballads and sensational Gothic novels sold like hot cakes. Scott hired a German tutor and was soon translating poems and plays. Aspects of his reading at this time coloured his later writing, notably his narrative poems and the novel *The Bride of Lammermoor.*

Scott's apprenticeship was interrupted by illness. When he recovered, his father agreed that he should study for the Bar, which involved representing clients in court. After a period back at University studying Law, he began his career as an advocate in 1792. Although unsuccessful at the Bar, and despite his later fame as an author, Scott stuck with the Law. He became Sheriff-depute of Selkirkshire in 1799, and a Principal Clerk to the Court of Session from 1806 to 1830.

Meanwhile the French Revolution had broken out, and in 1793 Britain went to war with France. Invasion was feared, and a part-time volunteer force was formed to defend Edinburgh from attack. Scott was desperate to join, and mortified to be turned down because he couldn't march. Only in 1797, with the formation of the Edinburgh Volunteer Light Dragoons, was he accepted as a Lieutenant of Horse. Scott loved military life, made friends with titled young men and wore his uniform long after the regiment was disbanded.

Around 1790, Scott had fallen in love with Williamina Belches, the only child of a wealthy, titled couple. Neither set of parents approved of a marriage between an heiress and an unsuccessful advocate, and Scott was deeply disappointed when, in 1796, Williamina dropped him and married someone else. Although he claimed to be heartbroken, a year later he married Margaret Charlotte Carpenter, an anglicised French woman whom he had met on holiday in Cumbria. They had four children.

For the rest of his life, Scott combined his legal work with a career as a best-selling writer. He was fortunate in his first publisher: Archibald Constable was an astute talent-spotter who paid huge advances on commercially promising work. As Scott grew rich, his lifestyle became extravagant, leading him to embark on what would prove a risky enterprise. Secretly – because 'gentlemen' did not associate themselves with trade – he went into partnership with James Ballantyne, a Kelso-born printer whom he had known since boyhood. Insisting that all his own work must be printed by Ballantyne & Co., and using his contacts to secure other jobs, Scott pocketed half the profits of the printing works.

At first all went well. Scott bought a fine house in Edinburgh's New Town and in 1812 began to build Abbotsford, his 'romance in stone' by the river Tweed near Melrose. Over the next fourteen years the house was enlarged in a style incorporating Scott's passions for medievalism, romanticism and Gothic imagery. He began to call himself the Laird of Abbotsford, and in 1820 received a knighthood from King George IV.

Almost inevitably, Scott's prodigality turned out badly. By 1818 his health had deteriorated; his lame leg troubled him and he had debilitating, painful spells of illness, probably caused by gallstones. In 1826 an economic and financial crisis affected all of Britain. Both Constable and Ballantyne went bankrupt and Scott, finding himself responsible for the printer's debts as well as his own, seemed likely to follow. Because he had passed nominal ownership of Abbotsford to his elder son in 1825, Scott was able to live there, but was obliged to sell his Edinburgh house and give control of his affairs to a Board of Trustees. His secret association with Ballantyne became public, and the humiliation affected him deeply.

During his remaining seven years of life, Scott worked tirelessly to pay off his debts (estimated at £126,000, approximately £6,000,000 today). He wrote night and day, essays, articles, biographies and novels, their quality deteriorating as his mental and physical health gave way. He suffered two strokes in 1830 and a third in early 1831.

Scott's last years were also darkened by a political storm engulfing the entire United Kingdom. Ever since the French Revolution and the violent Terror in Paris, he had had a horror of mob rule, believing that any movement away from rule by landowners and aristocracy would lead to civil disorder and social disintegration. By the end of the Napoleonic Wars, however, ordinary people were tired of the old order, and groups of Radicals, mostly returning soldiers and working men, began to agitate for the right to vote.

Of the two official political parties, the more progressive and liberal Whigs were sympathetic to such aspirations, while the ruling Tories, keenly supported by Scott, reacted angrily to any expression of Radical views. As an officer in the Light Dragoons, Scott had helped to break up minor riots in the 1800s, but only after 1819, when the government banned trades unions and public meetings, and demonstrations were inflated by Tory propaganda into 'Radical Wars', did his attitude harden into a phobia of even minimal political reform.

In 1830 the Whigs came to power, and immediately introduced a Reform Bill to Parliament. This was passed in 1832, extending the franchise somewhat – though most British citizens still did not have the right to vote. Scott's raucous opposition to reform lost him friends. He wrote an incendiary pamphlet (wisely turned down by his publisher), made contemptuous speeches, and in 1831 he was spat on and stoned in Jedburgh by furious protesters. For a man proud of his popularity, such disrespect was hard to bear.

Later that year, to avoid another harsh Scottish winter, Scott embarked with his son and daughter on a cruise from Southampton to Malta and Naples. There, in April 1832, overcome with homesickness, he began a gruelling journey back across the Alps and along the river Rhine. At Nijmegen on the Dutch border he suffered a devastating stroke and, although he made it back to Abbotsford, the end of Scott's life was marred by extreme disability and mental disturbance. He died on 21 September 1832, three months after the Reform Act became law.

2. SCOTT'S POETRY AND PROSE

Although best known for his novels, Scott's writing encompassed a variety of forms. His first serious publication was *Minstrelsy of the Scottish Border*, a collection of ballads drawn mainly from oral sources he had known in childhood, but incorporating some from English tradition and 'imitations' by himself and others. Its success inspired him to write his own poetry, and between 1805 and 1810 he published the three works that established his reputation, *The Lay of the Last Minstrel*, *Marmion* and *The Lady of the Lake*. These long story-poems all had Scottish themes, drawing on history, legend and romance. *The Lady of the Lake*, set around Loch Katrine in the Trossachs, was particularly popular, and is credited with kickstarting the Scottish tourist industry.

The Lady of the Lake was also the zenith of Scott's career as a poet. Overtaken in the popularity stakes by a younger poet, the dazzlingly romantic and morally dubious George Gordon, Lord Byron (1788–1824), middle-aged Scott accepted that in the world of poetry he was yesterday's man. He continued to write poems but increasingly turned his attention to prose. It is worth noting, however, the beautiful short lyrics woven into Scott's novels, and the subtle way he uses them to suggest traits of character – as in 'Lucy Ashton's Song' from the third chapter of *The Bride of Lammermoor*.

In 1805 the London publisher John Murray invited Scott to complete an unfinished novel by an English antiquarian, Joseph Strutt (1749–1802), titled *Queen-hoo Hall*. Intended as a romance illustrative of fifteenth-century manners and customs, the completed work, published in 1808, flopped disastrously. The task, however, had taught Scott about the use of language in fiction: Strutt, he wrote in the 'General Preface to the Waverley Novels' (1829), had 'rendered his language too ancient', and concluded that 'Every work designed for mere amusement must be expressed in language easily comprehended'. This may raise a wry smile in readers confronted by a Scott novel for the first time, because his notion of 'language easily comprehended' is so different from our own. But it is a good point. The reason Scott was so popular among his contemporaries was that he wrote according to the common usage of his time; if we find his mode of expression complex, it is because modern prose tends to be less discursive and conversation much less formal.

Scott's first novel was *Waverley*, an adventure story set mainly in the Highlands, in the period of the second Jacobite Rising in 1745–46. Published by Archibald Constable in 1814, it was a sensation. Scott, who delighted in obfuscation, withheld his name from the title page (as he would from every novel until 1827, receiving the ironic title 'The Great Unknown'), but readers of *The Lady of the Lake* were not easily deceived.

During the next eighteen years, Scott wrote twenty-six novels and several shorter stories. As his health declined seriously, there was a sad falling-off in quality and the 'English novels', set mainly in the medieval period, now have limited popular appeal – with the notable exception of *Ivanhoe*, which is still the most adapted of his novels. The modern consensus is that Scott's reputation rests on a handful of 'Scottish novels', notably *Waverley*, *Guy Mannering* (1815), *The Antiquary* (1816), *Old Mortality* (1816), *Rob Roy* (1817), *The Heart of Midlothian* (1818), *The Bride of Lammermoor* (1819), and *Redgauntlet* (1824). In these Scott's knowledge of his country's history, his evocation of landscape, familiarity with the old Scots language, narrative skill and sympathetic handling of characters establish his claim to be Scotland's greatest writer.

The few decades on either side of 1800 saw a great flourishing of literary magazines, both in Edinburgh and London. *The Edinburgh Review*, *Blackwood's Magazine* and *The Quarterly Review* were pre-eminent, and Scott wrote for all of them –

lengthy reviews and articles on everything from medieval chivalry to landscape gardening. He also wrote pamphlets on current affairs, notably the *Letters of Malachi Malagrowther*, a caustic response to the intention, in 1826, of the Bank of England to prohibit Scottish banks from printing their own £1 notes. Scott saw this as an attack on Scottish liberty and against Scotland's interest, and his pamphlet was widely credited with persuading the Bank of England to back off. In recognition of Scott's help, the Bank of Scotland put his portrait on their banknotes, where it remains to this day.

In 1826, the year in which his wife died and his financial affairs unravelled, Scott began to keep a journal, and continued with few interruptions until his death in 1832. Aware that it would be posthumously published, he might have been tempted to massage his self-image, and defend himself from public criticism sparked by the revelation of his financial indiscretion. Instead he wrote with searing honesty about his feelings of pain and humiliation, 'the cold sinkings of despair' as his world crumbled and his health failed. At the same time, the *Journal* is full of the humour and interest in humanity which made Scott loved in his lifetime. Published most recently in a scholarly yet accessible volume edited by W. E. K. Anderson (1988), *The Journal of Sir Walter Scott* has as great a claim to classic status as any of his other works.

3. *THE BRIDE OF LAMMERMOOR*: A GOTHIC NOVEL?

The Bride of Lammermoor frequently appears in lists of Gothic novels, stretching from Horace Walpole's seminal *The Castle of Otranto* (1765) to modern-day vampire novels. To judge how well *The Bride* fits into this remarkably resilient genre, it is helpful to know where its ideas originated, and what it meant in Scott's lifetime.

The second half of the eighteenth century saw a movement among younger European writers, away from the Neoclassical style, with its respect for Greek and (particularly) Roman models and strict rules of composition, towards a more natural form of expression. An important concern was the definition of what separated 'the sublime' from what was merely beautiful, particularly as it affected the human response to nature and landscape. Ordered, pastoral scenery that appealed to the eye was usually considered beautiful, but to achieve sublimity other elements were required. These were famously stated in Edmund Burke's *A Philosophical Inquiry into the Origin of Our Ideas of the Sublime and the Beautiful* (1746) and included vastness, solitude, terror, horror, awe (with its supernatural and religious connotations) and pain – reactions evoked by desolate mountains, howling winds and icy wastes rather than pretty cottage gardens. Burke's conclusion was that 'Whatever is in any sort terrible is a source of the *sublime*, that is, it is productive of the strongest emotion which the mind is capable of feeling'.

A Philosophical Inquiry was a key text for a younger generation, touching art, music and literature. The movement, known as Romanticism, celebrated human emotions, was protective of the natural environment and sensitive to spiritual or supernatural elements in the individual's experience. Its first English exponents were Wordsworth, whose poetic aim was 'to use the real language of men in a state of vivid sensation', and his friend Coleridge, whose poem *The Rime of the Ancient Mariner* covers most of Burke's definitions of 'the sublime'. Scott shared a similar outlook; his description of wild landscape, use of the common tongue and exploration of his characters' emotions were all Romantic traits.

Romanticism was a thoughtful, intellectual response to Burke's ideas, but his work also inspired a wilder, more melodramatic reaction, a kind of extreme Romanticism loosely known as 'Gothic'. The name derived from the perpendicular architectural style of the Middle Ages, with its vertiginous towers and dimly lit, echoing stone chambers. Taking its cue from the most sensational of Burke's definitions, horror, terror and the supernatural, Gothic writing is well summed up in the German term *Schauerroman*, a 'shudder novel'. Such stories were usually set in the past (often the Middle Ages), in the deeply forested regions of southern Europe. They centred on monasteries, brooding castles and dungeons, with a cast of assassins, ghostly nuns, vampires and vengeful spectres. Although most European literatures were touched by the Gothic movement, it took its deepest root in Britain and Germany.

Gothic fiction was particularly fascinating to Scots, who had a deep interest in two of its key factors, the national past and its myths, and the intrusion of supernatural elements into everyday experience. Scottish writers abandoned European settings in favour of their own bleak mountains and murky towns, using their own local superstitions. In the nineteenth century alone, masterpieces such as James Hogg's *The Private Memoirs and Confessions of a Justified Sinner* (1824), Robert Louis Stevenson's *Strange Case of Dr Jekyll and Mr Hyde* (1886), and Margaret Oliphant's 'The Library Window' (1896), plug into a distinctively Scottish sense of an unstable borderland between the seen and the unseen. Despite such instances of literary excellence, however, many shallow, poorly-written 'shockers' gave Gothic a bad name, and the genre has sometimes been dismissed by the well-educated as lowbrow nonsense.

So is *The Bride of Lammermoor* a Gothic novel? It certainly ticks a lot of boxes. Its setting on a bleak, wind-raked coast, the ruinous tower of Wolf's Crag and the sinister, shivering quicksands of the Kelpie's Flow are standard Gothic motifs, while vengeful Edgar Ravenswood, predestined to be the last of his house, is a suitably dark, tortured figure. The horror evoked by the supernatural impinging on the humdrum is also a recurring Gothic theme. Yet to read *The Bride* simply as Gothic melodrama is to miss its greater strengths; its exploration of the minds of its characters and their capacity to change, its moral ambivalence and the question of whether fate can undermine human desires and freedom of will. In many respects it transcends the genre.

It is often pointed out that in the body of Scott's fiction, *The Bride* is a one-off. Although he had used Gothic devices freely in his poetry, his previous novels had been defined by grounded characters and actual events. He may have meant *The Bride* to follow similar lines, since it too has a historical counterpart. Always modestly anxious to share his sources with readers, Scott's stated intention was to base the story on one told by his mother and great-aunt – no doubt with spooky embellishments – by the fireside when he was a child. It concerned the family of Viscount Stair (1619–95), at a time when Scotland was involved in a bitter civil war between Presbyterians (Covenanters) and Royalists fighting on behalf of the Episcopalian King Charles II. Stair's daughter, Janet Dalrymple, was in love with an impoverished Royalist, Archibald, Lord Rutherfurd. Her parents refused to allow the engagement; Janet was forced into an arranged marriage with David Dunbar of Baldoon in Wigtonshire, and the wedding took place in the church at Old Luce in 1669. Unhinged by grief, the bride died shortly afterwards.

On the bones of this spare, unhappy tale, Scott constructed *The Bride of Lammermoor*, a complex narrative darkened by the primitive power of superstition over human minds, completely at odds with the rational tone of his other work. It is known that Scott was seriously ill and taking opiates during the period when he was composing *The Bride*. Although the story of his dictating the book to an amanuensis in a drug-induced trance is now discredited, it seems possible that the sense of despair in the narrative, as well as its highly coloured dramatic action and Gothic elements, owed something to the author's temporarily altered state of mind.

4. TIME, PLACE AND THE SUPERNATURAL

A) HISTORICAL BACKGROUND

Although the main themes of *The Bride of Lammermoor* are romantic and tragic, Scott anchors his story in a particular time and place. Thus the novel is more easily read with some knowledge of the historical period in which the characters, notably Sir William Ashton and the Ravenswoods, play out their roles. The Oxford World's Classics edition, edited by Fiona Robertson (on which this *Scotnote* is based) contains an appendix (pp. 357–62) which deals with the history in detail; what follows is a summary of the main events preceding the action of the book.

The key event of the sixteenth century in Europe was the Reformation of the Christian Church, which caused a schism between those who chose to remain Roman Catholics and 'Protestants' who embraced a more radical theology. The Protestant Church of England retained some features of Catholicism, crucially the role of bishops. In Scotland, the Reformation of the 1560s cut more deeply into the structure of the national church, which was reorganised along more egalitarian lines. Some sacraments were scrapped and bishops were banned, replaced by ministers and 'elders'; congregations were grouped in presbyteries, hence the name 'Presbyterian'.

Queen Elizabeth of England's cousin, James VI of Scotland (1566–1625) succeeded her to the English throne in 1603, to reign as James VI and I. Settling in London, he ruled Scotland through a committee of lawyers and noblemen, the Privy Council. Brought up Presbyterian, James joined the Church of England, disappointing Scots with his famous slogan, 'No bishop, no king'. This attitude was taken further by his son, Charles I (1600–49), whose belief in the 'divine right' of kings to ignore Parliament and impose their preferred form of religion on their subjects led to conflict. Despite two Covenants drawn up to protect the Presbyterian church, Charles's attempts to impose bishops and a formal prayer book on the Church of Scotland caused two 'Bishops' Wars' (1639–40).

In 1642, the King's contempt for Parliament precipitated the outbreak of the Wars of the Three Kingdoms. The Scots became involved. The terms 'Royalist' and 'Cavalier', 'Parliamentarian' and 'Roundhead' belong to this period. In England, Royalists were usually Roman Catholic or 'Highchurch' Episcopalian, while the Puritan opposition was drawn from various Protestant sects. Among Scots, Highland Catholic chiefs and their clans mainly favoured the king, while the Lowlanders were mostly Presbyterian. Charles I was captured and executed in 1649. The Scots proclaimed his son, Charles II, as their king, in exchange for his promise to support the Presbyterian religion. This defiance was in vain; Charles was driven into exile and Scotland defeated by the English armies of Oliver Cromwell, who ruled both kingdoms until his death in 1658. Scotland's affairs were first handled by eight commissioners appointed by the English Parliament, then, from 1655, by a council of State, consisting of seven Englishmen and two Scots.

The restoration of Charles II in 1660 again disappointed Scots, to whom he had promised religious freedom. Episcopacy was forced on them, ministers and congregations lost their churches, and field meetings or conventicles became common among beleaguered Presbyterians. In *The Bride* (ch. 24 pp. 257–59), Allan, Lord Ravenswood, is depicted as leading a band of his vassals on the Royalist side at the bloody battle of Bothwell Bridge (1679).

In 1681, a Test Act required statesmen and clergymen to swear an oath recognising the King's authority in spiritual as well as secular affairs. Neither Presbyterian nor Roman

Catholic could oblige, and so began the 'Killing Times' when Covenanters were hunted down and executed by Royalist troops under General John Graham of Claverhouse, Viscount Dundee (1648–89), widely known as 'Bloody Clavers'. This cruel persecution is alluded to in *The Bride* by the clergyman Mr Bide-the-Bent (ch. 31 p. 315).

In 1685, Charles II was succeeded by his brother, a Roman Catholic convert, as King James VII of Scotland and II of England. Like his grandfather Charles I, James ignored Parliament, and was widely suspected of plotting to foist his religious beliefs on his subjects. The birth in 1688 of a Catholic heir (James Edward Stuart, the 'Old Pretender') and intensified antagonism between King and Parliament led seven English aristocrats to invite the King's Dutch Protestant son-in-law, William, Prince of Orange (1650–1702) to lead an army into England. William landed in Devon, and James fled to France with his wife and son. William and his wife, James's Protestant daughter, became King William III and Queen Mary II. The following year they were offered the Crown of Scotland as well, which they accepted.

Not everyone was pleased. A 'Glorious Revolution' to some was to others a wicked betrayal of the Stuart kings' God-given right to rule. A largely Catholic and Episcopalian pro-James rising in the Highlands, led by Graham of Claverhouse, defeated a force of William's supporters at Killiecrankie (1689). But Claverhouse died in the battle and, bereft of its leader, the insurrection fizzled out. In *The Bride*, Allan, Lord Ravenswood, fights with Claverhouse, is convicted of treason and stripped of his title (ch. 2 pp. 26–27). Sir William Ashton, Presbyterian and middle-class, prospers politically and financially under William and Mary, enabling him to buy the disgraced Ravenswood's estate.

In 1690, James Stuart was routed by William III in Ireland, at the Battle of the Boyne. James returned to France where, with the permission of King Louis XIV, he established a court-in-exile at Saint-Germain-en-Laye near Paris, referred to in *The Bride* as St Germains. Here the 'Jacobites' (supporters of *Jacobus*, Latin for James) plotted their comeback. Secret agents such as Captain Craigengelt (ch. 6 p. 70) were sent to Britain to gather information and recruits, and a mini-revolt was staged in 1708. The last serious risings in support of the Stuarts took place in 1715 and 1745–46.

The action of *The Bride* takes place before these events, during the reign of Queen Anne (1665–1714), who succeeded William III in 1702. By then Scotland was little more than a satellite state. Career politicians like Sir William Ashton had gained power at the expense of the old aristocracy, represented by the Ravenswoods. Feudal loyalties in the Lowlands were loosening. The situation is illustrated (ch. 12 pp. 138–40), when the faithful servant Caleb Balderstone clashes with the lawyer Davie Dingwall over the duty owed to the Master of Ravenswood by the inhabitants of Wolf's-hope, and Girder the cooper appeals to Ashton, rather than Ravenswood, for a vacant government post. Popular disgruntlement surfaces again in the conversation (ch. 24 pp. 256–61) of Ravenswood and the straight-talking sexton Mortsheugh, and in the bitter remarks of the three 'hags' at Lucy's funeral (ch. 35 pp. 341–42).

There has been some scholarly debate about the date of the novel's action, arising from discrepancies between the original 1819 version and the *Magnum Opus* ('Great Work') edition revised by Scott in 1830. In it he shifted the action from the end of the seventeenth century to the period just after the Union of Parliaments (1707). This decision caused inconsistencies, not all of which Scott rectified; post-1707, for example, Sir William Ashton could not have been Keeper of the Great Seal of Scotland, a post abolished at the Union. The variations between the two versions are of interest to scholars, and may be spotted by historically-informed readers, but do not interfere with appreciation or understanding of the book.

B) THE SETTING

Janet Dalrymple's doomed love for Archibald, Lord Rutherfurd was played out in the south-west of Scotland, around Stranraer. For *The Bride*, Scott chose to relocate the scene to the east (the Lammermuir Hills are south of Edinburgh). The action takes place in the coastal region of East Lothian and Berwickshire, with its bleak winter cliffs, watery skies and insistently thudding waves. Here Scott placed the half-ruined stronghold of Wolf's Crag, a 'solitary and naked tower, situated on a projecting cliff that beetled on the German Ocean' (ch. 7 p. 83). This was the last shelter of Edgar, disinherited heir of the Ravenswoods and doomed suitor of Lucy Ashton, the eponymous Bride. By setting almost the entire narrative in this lonely, sea-washed region, contrasting it only with the better-maintained but brooding Ravenswood Castle muffled in its forest cloak, Scott creates a claustrophobic yet untamed environment, where ancient superstitions still form the mindset of an isolated community, and the uncompromising landscape is a fearful metaphor for nature's indifference to human pain.

C) THE SUPERNATURAL

The supernatural is a device rarely used by Scott; he was one of many educated Scots fascinated by myth, legend and symbol, but who do not seriously believe in the existence – outside the human imagination – of paranormal phenomena. What distinguishes *The Bride* from the crude, shock-horror type of Gothic fiction is Scott's perception of the psychological effect of superstition on the minds of those who do believe in it – unsophisticated people living close to nature in a dark corner of the world. Caleb believes in the prophecy of the sinister Kelpie's Flow; her neighbours believe in the occult powers of Ailsie Gourlay; Blind Alice is suspected of witchcraft; Lucy takes pleasure in the legends of the Ravenswoods until her already unstable mind is poisoned by Gourlay's evil perversion of them. More worldly types like the Marquis of A——, Sir William and Lady Ashton and Bucklaw are untroubled, while modern, educated Ravenswood scoffs – until, under unbearable stress, he hears his future horribly predicted by the old women in Alice's garden (ch. 23 pp. 250–52). Then rationality deserts him, and he accepts the fate predicted for him by legend and prophecy.

To see the novel in psychological terms does not detract from the power of the supernatural elements to unsettle the reader's imagination – not unnaturally, for they surface from the deep folk memory of our race. The bitter old hags, overheard by Ravenswood spelling out his doom (ch. 23 pp. 250–52) are witches of nightmare. The story of the Mermaiden's Fountain (ch. 5 pp. 57–59) is a portent of punishment to the Ravenswoods. The bull killed by Ravenswood (ch. 5 p. 56), the emblem of his family, is an ancient symbol of sex and fertility, both denied to the young lovers. The blood-drenched raven falling dead at their feet (ch. 20 p. 209) is a bird long associated with ill fortune and an omen of pending disaster. Yet even as we are drawn imaginatively into this lurid world, we are aware of the sober truth, that the tragedy of *The Bride* is down to historical enmity, human intransigence, wickedness and pride.

5. STRUCTURE AND LANGUAGE

A) STRUCTURE

After the anonymous publication of *Waverley* in 1814, Archibald Constable successfully promoted *Guy Mannering* and *The Antiquary* as 'By the Author of *Waverley*'. Two years later Scott, beset by financial difficulties, decided to try his luck with another publisher. He absolved himself from ratting on Constable by removing the reference to *Waverley* from the title page, but was still determined on anonymity. This led him, when agreeing a four-volume deal with William Blackwood and his London agent John Murray, to create an alias, a pedantic fictional schoolmaster named Jedediah Cleishbotham. The first stories for Blackwood, 'edited' by Cleishbotham, were supposedly written by his deceased colleague Peter Pattieson, who in turn had heard them from the owner of the Wallace-Head Inn in the village of Gandercleugh – hence the title *Tales of My Landlord*.

Modern readers tend to be irritated by this framing narrative, finding that it distracts from the actual story. With Scott's authorship known since 1827, the mystification and disguises seem tedious, and put paid to a punchy opening which grabs the reader on page one. The device should be noted, however, since *The Bride of Lammermoor*, published in 1819, is a component of *Tales of My Landlord* third series. In *The Bride*, the framing narrative is established in chapter 1, which declares Peter Pattieson as the author who constructs the novel from a handful of notes and sketches given to him by Dick Tinto, an itinerant artist. The actual story of *The Bride* begins in chapter 2. It is tempting to skip the first chapter entirely, but serious students should read it, either before or after reading the rest of the book.

The overall structure is also affected by the way fiction was published in the eighteenth and nineteenth centuries. Instead

Walter Scott's *The Bride of Lammermoor*

of the lengthy one-volume novels of today, publication was in three or four separate volumes. In *Tales of My Landlord* third series, *The Bride of Lammermoor* occupied two-and-a-half volumes out of four; the remaining one-and-a-half contained *A Legend of Montrose*.

The first volume of *The Bride* ended with chapter 13 (p. 153), the second with chapter 27 (p. 291). These breaks enabled Scott, at the end of volume one, to leave the reader on a cliff-hanger and, at the end of volume two, to indicate a lapse of time before the climax of the action in the half-volume ending the story. There is also a marked difference in tone between the first volume and the rest of the book. Although a sense of impending doom colours the first part of the narrative, Scott is also concerned with establishing the identities, traits and relationships of his characters, and expounding the political and historical animosities behind the approaching tragedy. The suggestion of uncanniness becomes more intense in the second, with the revelation of the doom of the last Ravenswood (ch. 18 p. 185), the prophetic horror of blind Alice at the association of Edgar and Lucy (ch. 19 p. 199), the shooting of the raven (ch. 20 p. 209), the apparition of Alice to Ravenswood and the arrival of the three 'witches' (ch. 23 pp. 249–51). Scott used a structure imposed on him by a publishing convention to his own advantage in giving internal form to his book.

B) THE PREFACE OF 1830

In a sense, there is a second framing narrative providing structure to Scott's novel. Writing new introductions near the end of his life for the *Magnum Opus* edition, Scott insisted on revealing his sources. After his death, tracking down 'The Scott Originals' (the title of a book by W. S. Crockett published in 1912) and identifying the 'real places' he wrote about became a kind of sport among his fans. The fictional

Wolf's Crag, for instance, was identified as Fast Castle near St Abb's Head, as if this added something to understanding *The Bride*. In the 1830 introduction (Oxford edition pp. 1–11), Scott told at length the story of Janet Dalrymple and Lord Rutherfurd, feeding the notion that all he had to do was to change names and relate a historical incident (modern editorial approaches to Scott's novels, however, emphasise the importance of the original texts: in the 1995 Edinburgh Edition of the Waverley Novels of *The Bride of Lammermoor*, the editor returned to Scott's 1819 text, and omitted the 1830 introduction).

It cannot be emphasised too strongly that, just as a stage play is not a documentary, a novel is not simply a retelling of a real-life story. It may be interesting to know what sparked an idea, but a modern reading of a novel insists on an examination of the text: how Scott describes and explores the minds of his characters and creates a credible world for them to live in; how he creates dramatic tension; his use of dialogue and how effectively he enriches the narrative by the use of symbols and elements suggesting the workings of primitive powers.

C) THE *ROMEO AND JULIET* COMPARISON

The Bride of Lammermoor has often been paired with Shakespeare's tragedy of doomed young love, and certain aspects of the story invite comparison. Both are tragedies of fate. The enmity of two families whose son and daughter are destined to fall in love, the determination of parents to thwart them, the fact that all around them are driven by their own greedy ambition and see the young couple as pawns in a grown-up game give the two works a structural similarity. The novel has other Shakespearean echoes. Three 'witches' appear in both *Macbeth* and *The Bride*, and Ravenswood's conversation with the sexton (ch. 24 pp. 254–60) recalls the encounter of the prince with two gravediggers in *Hamlet*,

Prince of Denmark. Scott uses verses from *Romeo and Juliet* as epigrams to chapters 5 and 33.

The difference is, however, greater than the similarity. A play is written to be performed; dialogue and physical interaction alone must evoke the actors' inner experience. The novelist is free to explore thoughts and motivations, and Scott devotes a large portion of his narrative to the conflicts in his characters' minds, their awareness of class difference, shifting loyalties and unpromising incompatibility of temperament. Although Edgar and Lucy are young, they are too clear-sighted, their passion too tortured to allow them even a transitory illusion of 'happiness ever after'. The hopelessness of their struggle to hold together in the face of evil intent is evident all along.

D) SCOTT'S USE OF LANGUAGE

For first-time readers of Scott, his use of eighteenth-century language can be daunting. Modern writing is, in general, tauter and less discursive, sentences shorter and ideas more concisely expressed. Scott, educated in Latin, naturally used constructions which today may seem ponderous, and a latinate vocabulary containing words and phrases now less familiar. Scott's prose was also influenced by the rhythms of the sixteenth-century King James Bible, familiar to most Scots until the 1960s; *The Bride* is full of references to this text (carefully explained in the editor's notes) which echo in the speech patterns of his characters – again, less familiar than in the past. For a new reader, the best advice is to persevere. Once his style becomes familiar, the power of Scott's writing, his storytelling genius and his exploration of character and motive make the effort rewarding.

It is worth noticing that in *The Bride*, as in his other novels, Scott tends to define social class through language, putting English into the mouths of his aristocratic characters and reserving Scots for those less refined. (The exception to this is Alice Gray, an Englishwoman by birth, whose speech emphasises her 'otherness' and slight social superiority to her fellow-retainers.) The distinction is a useful authorial device but, in fact, until the late eighteenth-century Enlightenment made English fashionable, Scots was spoken by rich and poor, educated and uneducated. Scott's posh characters have often been ridiculed for their stilted speech, and it is true that by comparison the Scots language used in *The Bride* by Caleb Balderstone, Johnnie Mortsheugh, the Girders and the 'witches' is wonderfully pithy and vigorous. With the spread of English as the language of the educated, much old Scots vocabulary has fallen out of use, and modern editions of Scott contain a glossary of words that his earlier Scottish readers would not have required.

6. THE FRAMING NARRATIVE: CHARACTERS AND THEME

Peter Pattieson and Dick Tinto
These characters appear only in chapter 1, devised by Scott to hide his authorship by establishing Peter Pattieson, schoolmaster of Gandercleugh and keen transcriber of folktales and legends, as author of *The Bride of Lammermoor*. The only mention in this book of Jedediah Cleishbotham, Pattieson's pompous editor, is in Scott's note 26, p. 355. Pattieson's voice as commentator is occasionally heard, e.g. on p. 245 and p. 282. Pattieson and his acquaintance Dick Tinto represent different types of artist familiar to Scott. To Pattieson, a teacher with a secure salary, writing is a leisure activity, whereas Tinto has chosen to live by his art. Unfortunately, he is not very good at it.

Pattieson begins by disclaiming desire for fame or personal aggrandisement (pp. 12–13), echoing Scott's professed view of celebrity. He next relates the story of Dick Tinto, whose early ambition exceeds his talent; he provokes derision by drawing a horse perceived to have five legs (p. 15). Later he becomes an itinerant portrait painter who, although uneasily aware of his limitations, makes a virtue of sharing art with everybody: 'And wherefore limit to the rich and higher classes alone the delight which the exhibition of works of art is calculated to inspire into all classes?' (p. 19). This is laudable (and strangely modern), but soon a dearth of patrons reduces Dick to the status of 'an out-of-doors artist' – his defiant term for a painter of inn signs – lowering his lofty standards to make ends meet.

Much of this narrative is funny, though the theme of a dedicated artist's descent into destitution is not treated lightly. The comedy also overlies serious artistic concerns. In an encounter at the Wallace-Head inn at Gandercleugh, where

Tinto has been engaged to paint a new inn sign, Pattieson and Tinto discuss (p. 21ff) whether writing, with its balance of dialogue and description, or art, with its visual impact, is the superior medium of communication. Connection with *The Bride* is established in this conversation. In support of his own conviction that painting is greater, Tinto shows Pattieson a preliminary sketch he has made for a 'history-piece', featuring a quarrel between characters dressed in mid-seventeenth-century costume, in a room furnished in the style of the mid-sixteenth. This draws criticism from scholarly Pattieson, brushed aside by Dick, to whom historical accuracy is irrelevant. The subject, he says, is drawn from a tale he heard from an old peasant woman who guided him round an (unnamed) castle, informing him that her story 'was by tradition claimed to be truth, although, as upwards of a hundred years had passed away since the events took place, some doubts upon the accuracy of all the particulars might be reasonably entertained' (p. 23). As a comment on the relationship between history and myth, these are pertinent words.

Although to the artist's fury Pattieson fails to read a story in the sketch, he subsequently used Dick's notes, 'a parcel of loose scraps [...] where outlines of caricatures, sketches of turrets, mills, old gables and dovecots, disputed the ground with his written memoranda' (p. 25) as inspiration for *The Bride*. In Pattieson's literary version, the inconsistencies of Tinto's are ironed out and the narrative anchored in a specific historical period. But speaking through him, Scott uses the framing-narrative to voice his own opinion of storytelling – that oral traditions may be inaccurately transcribed and narrators unreliable, their prejudices and misjudgements – as well as imaginative licence – fatally skewing their versions of the past. This throws light on the ambiguities and shifting points of view that prove disturbing in the novel, making it both dreamlike and luridly real.

The framing narrative also gives insight into Scott's knowledge of, and interest in, art. *The Bride* contains detailed descriptions of portraiture, used to suggest character traits and the social class of its subjects (pp. 191–92; pp. 281–82).

7. SUMMARY OF CHAPTERS 2–35

Ch. 2. The narrative opens with a description of the coastal landscape of East Lothian, and the Ravenswoods' association with it. Sir William Ashton and his family are introduced. The history of the antagonism between the aristocratic, Jacobite-supporting Ravenswoods and Sir William, a middle-class lawyer brought to power by the 'Glorious Revolution' of 1688–89, is explained. The funeral of Allan, Lord Ravenswood, is next described (p. 31ff), using the chilly Gothic imagery that will recur throughout the text: a misty November morning, the half-ruinous Wolf's Crag, the banners and black clothing of the mourners, the dreary chapel where the body will be buried by proscribed Episcopalian rites. The local Presbyterian authority has asked Sir William to stop the service, leading to the presence of a law officer who, supported by armed men, orders the clergyman to desist. Edgar, Master of Ravenswood and son of the deceased, orders him to proceed; when the law officer attempts to enforce his will, the mourners draw their swords. The Master lowers the head of the coffin 'into the charnel vault' (p. 33), then makes an indignant speech, blaming Sir William Ashton for the disruption of the funeral, and Lord Ravenswood's death. Some applaud, but 'the more cool and judicious' present regret such a public declaration. The lavish funeral feast at Wolf's Crag, which will beggar the Master, is consumed among insults to the Lord Keeper and friendly assurances to Ravenswood. His guests gone, Ravenswood returns to the hall which he imagines full of phantoms representing 'the tarnished honour and degraded fortunes of his house, the destruction of his own hopes, and the triumph of that family by whom they had been ruined' (p. 34). Now comes the first suggestion of superstition in the tale. A peasant (in this context a credulous, uneducated person) might afterwards affirm that 'on this fatal night the Master of Ravenswood […]

evoked some evil fiend, under whose malignant influence the future tissue of incidents was woven' (p. 35).

Ch. 3. In the extravagantly refurbished library of Ravenswood Castle the Lord Keeper, having heard the law officers' account of the funeral and the threats made against him, is preparing a report for the Privy Council. Pondering his options in dealing with young Ravenswood, he glances up and sees on the ceiling the Ravenswoods' coat-of-arms, a black bull's head with the motto *I bide my time*, an uncomfortable reminder of Malisius (elsewhere called Malise) de Ravenswood, who killed a usurper of his lands in the thirteenth century (p. 38). Hearing his daughter singing, he shelves his report and invites her to walk in the wood. They are met by the forester Norman, who disparages the Ashtons' indifference to country pursuits and praises the Ravenswoods' hunting skills. Despite his displeasure, Sir William over-tips Norman, showing his inexperience in managing servants (p. 44). Unable to answer her father's questions about the Ravenswoods, Lucy suggests that they visit 'old Alice', a blind woman living in a tumbledown cottage nearby. Although advised by Lucy that Alice, a former nurse to the Ravenswoods, deplores their departure, Sir William agrees to visit her (p. 46).

Ch. 4. Unable to navigate his own property, city-bred Sir William is guided by Lucy through the wood. Alice's isolation and 'otherness' are emphasised by the overgrown thickets around the 'deep and obscure dell' where she sits under a tree outside her cottage. Alice is described, her cleanliness, dignity and English accent at odds with her lowly surroundings.

Conversation begins civilly, and they are served bread and honey from Alice's bees. Questioned by Sir William, Alice reveals that she has been sixty years on the estate, married a Scot and had six sons, now all dead (p. 50). The tone alters when Sir William mentions the decrepit condition of the cottage; when Lucy suggests that her father might improve it, the offer is abruptly declined. Sir William attempts to assure Alice that he bears her no ill-will for preferring the Ravenswoods, expressing the hope that she will continue to live rent-free in his property for her lifetime. Alice meets his condescension with a cool reminder that this was a condition of the estate's sale. The conversation becomes darker as Alice warns Sir William to avoid tangling with Edgar Ravenswood: 'Believe a true tale – they are a fierce house and there is danger in dealing with men when they become desperate' (p. 52). At first inclined to dismiss Alice's warning, Sir William becomes alarmed by the idea that Ravenswood might become violent, especially when Alice cites a notorious murder committed in Edinburgh by a relation of the Ravenswoods. This touches the Lord Keeper's secret terror of assassination. Muttering that he believes the Master to be an honourable man – but if he is not, then the execution of his kinsman should deter him (p. 53) – he abruptly leaves the scene.

Ch. 5. As they walk home, Sir William asks Lucy why she looks so pale. Unwilling to say, she claims to be nervous of cattle, the remnant of an ancient breed, grazing nearby. Just then a bull (symbolic of the Ravenswoods) runs bellowing towards them. Sir William tries to protect Lucy, but when she faints they are in real danger. Suddenly a shot rings out and the bull falls dead. Sir William glimpses an armed figure among the trees. When he approaches, Sir William asks him to carry Lucy to a nearby well while he goes for help.

There follows (p. 57–59) the legend of the 'Mermaiden's Fountain', supposedly once the haunt of a beautiful lady loved by the then Lord Ravenswood. They meet, always on (unlucky) Fridays, the lady appearing near the well, and disappearing when the nearby chapel bell tolls for evening service – too soon for Lord Ravenswood, who persuades the priest to delay ringing the bell. When the lady realises she has been tricked, she leaps into the water, disappearing in a pool of blood. As so often in *The Bride*, a prosaic explanation is offered alongside the sensational; people 'wiser than the vulgar' believe that the lady, 'a beautiful maid of plebeian rank' (p. 58) was the mistress of one Raymond Ravenswood and killed by him in a jealous fit – this distinction was not typical of Gothic fiction generally. Yet superstition insists strongly that the decay of the Ravenswoods dates from this event, and it is dangerous for a Ravenswood to frequent the well. In this ominous place, Lucy begins to recover and, afraid for her father, insists on going to find him. Reluctantly supported by the dark, well-dressed stranger, she walks homeward, bewildered by the man's rejection of thanks and unwillingness to meet Sir William. When they do meet, the stranger cuts short Sir William's gratitude by declaring, 'I am the Master of Ravenswood' (p. 62). Once home and much alone, Lucy thinks constantly of Ravenswood, remembering his 'native nobleness of countenance and form' and 'mien and features so romantic and so striking' (p. 63). Vague about his quarrel with her father and supposing herself capable of sympathy, she falls in love with an image of her own creation, becoming 'involved in those mazes of the imagination which are most dangerous to the young and the sensitive' (p. 64). Sir William, aware of his debt to Ravenswood, tones down the report he received about the funeral; back in Edinburgh, he surprises the Privy Council by preaching 'the necessity of using conciliatory measures' with hot-headed young men (p. 65). He writes high-minded letters, suggesting that burying the hatchet would be the best option (but significantly not to his wife). The astonishment of Sir William's colleagues in the Council is summed up in a cynical conversation among its members, including the Marquis of A—— (p. 67).

Ch. 6. At the inn at Tod's Den (elsewhere Tod's-hole) the same evening, a young squire, Frank Hayston of Bucklaw, and his disreputable friend Captain Craigengelt are drinking and awaiting Ravenswood's arrival. Their bickering suggests stress — in fact they are plotters afraid of discovery. It transpires that Craigengelt, an agent of the Jacobite court-in-exile, has recruited both Bucklaw and Ravenswood to engage with the Stuart cause. Bucklaw, in debt and short of money, has been lured by the promise of a commission in the 'Irish brigade' (p. 70), while Ravenswood is disaffected, poor and keen to escape problems at home. Craigengelt is pleased to have recruited Ravenswood, whom he dislikes, but whose style, courage and good breeding will impress his royal masters. The intention is to leave Scotland that night on a French ship waiting off the coast, the delay caused by Ravenswood, who has gone to the Castle to remonstrate with Sir William Ashton. Craigengelt is gleeful, hoping the encounter will end in Ravenswood's killing Sir William, making it impossible for him to return to Scotland. This alarms Bucklaw, afraid of being associated with a criminal act, and tension rises when Craigengelt goes to the stable and returns with the news that Ravenswood's best horse, kept in readiness, has accidentally injured itself. Ravenswood eventually appears, muffled in a cloak and looking dejected (p. 74). Needled by Craigengelt, he admits that he has seen Sir William, but refuses to say why his desire for vengeance has weakened. He says that he does not, after all, intend to go abroad that night. When Craigengelt objects, citing his expense and danger of discovery, Ravenswood haughtily offers him a purse of gold, a transaction vetoed by Bucklaw as dishonourable. Claiming 'friendship' however, earns Bucklaw a severe snub from Ravenswood, who calls Craigengelt 'an intriguing adventurer' and Bucklaw 'a hotheaded bully' (p. 76). When he rides off, Bucklaw follows: 'I will after him, for I have had more of his insolence than I can well digest.'

Ch. 7. Riding home on his spare horse, Ravenswood is overtaken by Bucklaw and challenged to a duel. Ravenswood replies indifferently to Bucklaw's bluster, saying that he has no quarrel with him, but, as Bucklaw insists, he dismounts and draws his sword. They fight (pp. 78–79), Ravenswood coolly and Bucklaw wildly. When Bucklaw slips and falls, Ravenswood spares his life and Bucklaw makes his peace. A village boy arrives with news from the inn that Craigengelt has been captured and Bucklaw should 'ride for it'. Bucklaw panics, fearful that Craigengelt will betray him, and Ravenswood offers him shelter at Wolf's Crag. On the road they discuss Ravenswood's reasons for teaming up with 'such a rogue as Craigengelt, and such a scapegrace as folk call Bucklaw' (p. 80). Ravenswood cites desperation but, declining to give a reason for his change of mind, asks Bucklaw why he associates with Craigengelt. Bucklaw reveals that he has gambled away his land, can get no more until his great-aunt dies, and has foolishly believed Craigengelt's exaggeration of his influence at St Germains. Ravenswood, despite previously threatening violence against Sir William, now says he only intended to 'upbraid him with his tyranny and its consequences' (p. 81) – an early sign of his changing feelings since encountering Lucy in the wood. Arrival at Wolf's Crag signals the first appearance of Caleb Balderstone and his absurd pretence that the house is well-provided and full of servants. He refuses entry to the young men, then claims that there is food for their horses, that the best silver is locked away and that the roof has collapsed because the slaters haven't come to mend it (p. 86). Passing through the dismal hall, uncleared since the funeral feast, Ravenswood leads Bucklaw to a small room with a fire. After more feigning on Caleb's part, the young men dine on mutton scraps and a heel of cheese. For drink, Caleb salvages the dregs of claret left over after the funeral, and Bucklaw goes to bed in the 'secret chamber' used in the past to hide fugitives.

Ch. 8. During the night, Ravenswood reflects that at least he is not to blame for his poverty; he inherited it from his father, and from his aristocratic blood. Rising, he prays, then wakes Bucklaw, asking how he slept. Bucklaw complains about the mattress, rats and lack of curtains. Before breakfast, Ravenswood offers Caleb his remaining gold, telling him to buy 'what is necessary for the family' (p. 94), meaning the family's honour. Caleb's preferred method is to ask for credit from Ravenswood's former tenants, but the Master says he still intends to leave Scotland and prefers to be free from debt. For several days, Caleb manages to put food on the table, its inadequacy compensated by the young men's amusement at his stratagems. Bucklaw, an outdoors man, quickly develops cabin-fever. He occupies himself with grooming his horse, but, when Ravenswood tires of fencing practice and board games, he becomes depressed. The Master thinks of Lucy Ashton and worries that he treated her too coldly. Shame induces him, 'as if by way of recompense, to invest her with more of grace and beauty than perhaps she could actually claim' (p. 96). Instead of leaving he hangs about, writing to his Jacobite-leaning kinsmen, including the Marquis of A——, using the delay in receiving replies as reason to stay. Rumours circulate about a change of government, giving Jacobite Tories in the Privy Council a numerical advantage over Sir William's Whigs, and endangering his job. Ravenswood receives a flowery letter from the Marquis, vaguely promising support but advising him to stay at home. Bucklaw thinks the Marquis is plotting an uprising; if so, Ravenswood sees no good reason to get involved.

Ch. 9. Next morning, Bucklaw is wildly excited because riders are mustering for a stag-hunt, and rushes off to saddle his horse. Ravenswood learns from Caleb that his neighbour Lord Bittlebrains has organised the hunt, and counters Caleb's indignation by pointing out that Lord Bittlebrains now owns the land. After a discussion of Ravenswood's wardrobe, comical but again emphasising his poverty (p. 105), Caleb reveals that there are ladies accompanying the hunt. Reluctantly Ravenswood rides out with Bucklaw, but feels humiliated that they are held back by his inferior horse. He is accosted by 'a well-mounted stranger' (p. 107), who offers him the use of his. Bucklaw impudently grabs the stranger's horse, telling Ravenswood to ride his instead, and speedily departs. Asked why he allowed this, the stranger tells Ravenswood that the horse belongs to someone who wants to befriend him, but refuses to give a name. The hunt, horrific to a modern sensibility, ends with the barbarous killing of the stag. According to custom, the huntsman offers the knife to a lady (wearing a riding mask to protect her complexion) and invites her to make the first cut. When she declines from 'terror, or perhaps her compassion' (p. 109), the task is hijacked by ill-mannered Bucklaw, who revels in 'slashing, cutting, hacking and hewing' while up to his elbows in blood (p. 111). Ravenswood, losing interest, rides away, pausing on high ground to look back at the sport which had once been the privilege of aristocrats, (by inference, not louts like Bucklaw). He is joined by an elderly man in scarlet cloak and slouched hat covering most of his face, who reveals that he is the owner of the fine horse before beginning to talk about the history of Wolf's Crag and its owners' decline. When he suggests that all may not be lost for the Ravenswoods, he is snubbed: 'I am the Master of Ravenswood, and you [...] must be sensible, that the next mortification after being unhappy, is the being loaded with undesired commiseration' (pp. 113–14). But the old man sticks close, and is presently joined by his daughter, the masked young lady. The approach of a thunderstorm compels Ravenswood, despite deep embarrassment, to offer them shelter at Wolf's Crag. Caleb is appalled. The dinner hour is approaching, and as usual there is no food. Fantastically, he pretends that the other servants have gone to watch the hunt.

Ravenswood silences him, reveals the true state of affairs to his guests and orders Caleb to take the horses to the stable. Into this sticky situation rides Bucklaw, with more than half the hunting party behind him. Caleb is furious, but reacts predictably: 'The deil be in me [...] if they shall beat me yet!' (p. 117).

Ch. 10. Seeing the principal guests riding towards Wolf's Crag, the huntsman has volunteered to send the venison there – an offer eagerly accepted by thoughtless Bucklaw. Caleb, realising the trouble this will cause when the hunters invade the castle, waits until Ravenswood has shown his guests into the tower, clears the courtyard and shuts the gate on the would-be revellers, including Bucklaw. Speaking through a shot-hole, he says that no one may enter while the Master is at dinner, and directs them to the inn at Wolf's-hope. Left inside by an oversight is the servant who had offered Ravenswood his horse. Taking Caleb's place, he announces Lord Bittlebrains' wish that all should go down to the inn and order drinks, for which he will pay. As they leave, cursing Ravenswood's meanness, Bucklaw again takes the huff, 'and every mingled feeling led him to break off the union which he had formed with the Master of Ravenswood' (p. 121). On arrival at the inn, Bucklaw meets Craigengelt, who gives him the welcome news that he is free and safe; Bucklaw borrows drink-money from him and once again they are best friends. At Wolf's Crag, Ravenswood conducts his guests to the hall. Caleb has cleared the funeral debris but the room is still desolate, made even darker by the brewing thunderstorm. The clanging of the gate outside alarms the stranger, who realises he has been separated from his servants. Ravenswood reassures him and asks the guests to identify themselves. Embarrassed, the old man shuffles and shivers as he removes his cloak and hat. Losing patience, Ravenswood answers for him: 'I perceive [...] that Sir William Ashton is unwilling to announce himself in the Castle of Wolf's Crag' (p. 124). Relieved, Sir William denies that he planned the visit, but admits that the storm has given him a longed-for opportunity to thank Ravenswood for saving his life, and his daughter's. Despite his attraction to Lucy and the feeling that he owes civility to guests, Ravenswood cannot forget that this man is his father's most bitter enemy. He is confused, but the impasse is solved when Sir William tells Lucy to 'lay aside your mask, and let us express our gratitude to the Master openly and barefaced' (p. 125). Overcome by her shy beauty, Ravenswood capitulates, giving her a ceremonial kiss – cue the breaking of the storm, lightning illuminating the figures of Lucy and Ravenswood and the coats-of-arms on the walls – then the castle-shaking thunder and the fainting of Lucy, thrusting her into Ravenswood's arms for a second time. It is now impossible for the guests to return to Bittlebrains-House. Ravenswood will have to accommodate them overnight. Just then Caleb rushes into the hall.

Ch. 11. Caleb's latest brainwave had been to hide the absence of dinner by smashing china in the kitchen and pretending that a feast was ruined by falling soot – the result of a lightning strike. His absurdity, contrasted with Ravenswood's 'restrained impatience' (p. 130) amuses Lucy, and her hilarity infects both Sir William and Ravenswood. Lucy teases Caleb, who responds indignantly, piling one ludicrous claim upon another, the Scots tongue rendering his speech particularly pithy. Eventually Sir William suggests that Caleb should team up with his manservant Lockhard, who 'is quite accustomed to accidents and contingencies of every kind' (p. 132), and that between them they can manage the present emergency. Ravenswood's offer of his purse is again rejected by Caleb, unable to understand that times have changed: 'what suld I do wi' your honour's purse on your ain grund? I trust we are no' tae pay for our ain?' (p 132). When Lockhard and Caleb leave, Sir William apologises for his laughter and, a convincing actor, continues to feign shyness. He appears 'at once pushed on by his desire of appearing friendly, and held back by the fear of intrusion' (p. 133). Moved by Sir William's appearance of sincerity, but still maintaining his reserved manner, Ravenswood goes to arrange the night's accommodation. Lucy is to have his bedroom, with Mysie, dressed in a black satin gown once owned by Ravenswood's grandmother, as lady's maid. Caleb is sent to tell Bucklaw that the secret chamber is needed for the Lord Keeper, and Lockhard to bring venison from the inn. Mysie offers the guests 'the produce of her little dairy' (p. 134), and as the storm recedes, night settles over Wolf's Crag.

Ch. 12. Beset by misgivings, Caleb sets out for Wolf's-hope. He fears Ravenswood's reaction when he hears that Bucklaw is offended by his exclusion; he wishes he had taken the purse; he is afraid to meet Bucklaw, especially drunk. More important, of course, is 'the honour of the family' and how to get supplies without involving Lockhard (p. 135). At the village, the inhabitants have managed, during the Ravenswoods' troubles, to claim ownership of their properties. No longer willing to supply Wolf's Crag for free (pp. 136–37), they have engaged a lawyer, Davie Dingwall, to spell out the new position to Caleb (pp. 138–39). Now Caleb must either lose face before Lockhard by admitting Wolf's Crag's inability to provide dinner (unthinkable) or trust to villagers' compassion (improbable). Otherwise, because 'necessity was equally imperious and lawless' (p. 140), he will have to steal. Sending Lockhard to the inn, he goes to the house of Girder the cooper, where a christening feast is being prepared – though aware that Girder, a leader of the anti-Ravenswood faction, is unlikely to co-operate. He has more hope of Girder's wife and mother-in-law, Jean Lightbody of Loup-the-Dyke farm, with whom he had flirted when young. The contrast between the destitution of Wolf's Crag and the prosperity of the cooper's cottage appears in the women's finery, tablecloths, and fine food (p. 142). Caleb is warmly welcomed; the death of the Queen's cooper is mentioned, and they gossip about Ravenswood and Miss Ashton (pp. 144–45). But Caleb's interest is in wild-fowl being cooked on a spit by the cooper's apprentice. When the women are distracted by the baby's crying, he sends the boy on an errand and steals the birds. At the inn, he leaves a curt message telling Bucklaw to find a bed elsewhere. Craigengelt suggests pursuing Caleb, but Lockhard forbids this.

Ch. 13. At the Girders' cottage, the theft is discovered as Girder arrives with the minister, Mr Bide-the-bent, who tries to intervene when the furious Girder threatens violence: 'Am I no to chastise my ain wife?' is the cooper's astonished reply (p. 149). Only when he hears that Peter Puncheon, the Queen's cooper, is dead and the Lord Keeper is at Wolf's Crag does he calm down, realising that Caleb might be a useful go-between. He sends his foreman after Caleb who is stunned, when overtaken just short of the Castle, to be met, not with abuse, but with politeness and a gift of wine and brandy. When the foreman explains that Girder has an eye on Puncheon's job, and that a word to Sir William would be seen as a favour, Caleb replies loftily: 'Your master has acted with becoming civility [...] and I will not fail to represent it properly to my Lord Ravenswood' (p. 153).

Ch. 14. Caleb has gathered more food and drink than Wolf's Crag has seen since the funeral. While he spreads the tablecloth and lays out the venison and wildfowl, he boasts to Lockhard of the grandeur of past times. Lockhard remarks that the tenants at Ravenswood Castle are a difficult lot; Caleb agrees, but suggests they are worse now due to the change of master. He mentions 'prophecies about this house I wad like ill to see fulfilled', which Lockhard, who is not a local man, dismisses as 'freits' [superstitions]. He remarks that Ravenswood and Lucy make a winsome couple, but warns that 'there is a leddy sits in our hall-neuk maun have her hand in that' – a reference to the absent Lady Ashton (p. 155). Upstairs in the hall, Ravenswood is playing the courteous host. Though aware that his feelings are due to Lucy's charm and Sir William's plausible conversation, he is grateful to them for ignoring the state of the house, and for the respect they show for his 'high birth'. When the time comes for the guests to retire to rooms 'decored' by Mysie, the Lord Keeper sees off the overly servile Caleb, but detains Ravenswood, broaching the subject of his dispute with the late Lord Ravenswood. Citing his own suffering, as well as Lord Ravenswood's, he suggests that if the latter had agreed to a face-to-face meeting, an accommodation might have been found to benefit them both. He would, he suggests, have forfeited part of his legal right to be 'spared the pain of parting in enmity from a person whose general character I so much admired and honoured' (p. 159). Ravenswood claims proudly that neither he nor his father would have expected anything 'on the footing of favour', but Sir William continues: 'Can you blame me, an old man desirous of peace, and in the castle of a young nobleman who has saved my daughter's life and my own, that I am desirous [...] that these [disputes] should be settled on the most liberal principles?' (p. 159–60). Ravenswood's feelings are conflicted; he spends a sleepless night, unable now to forgive Sir William or pursue his vendetta against him. 'This man may be other than I have thought him', he concludes, 'and his daughter – but I have resolved not to think of her' (p. 160).

Ch. 15. The Lord Keeper cannot sleep either. Lying on a hard bed, he thinks of past and future. Alert to political change and adroit at exploiting it, he knows he is valued more for his legal knowledge than his trustworthiness. Now the Marquis of A——'s attempt to alter the balance of the Privy Council in his own favour seems close to success, but he still needs votes, and wants the Lord Keeper on his side. Through an agent, the Marquis has learned Sir William's greatest fear, since his interview with blind Alice – personal attack by the Master of Ravenswood. Seeing his chance to alarm Sir William further, he has the agent inform him that, under the Treaty of Union, the British House of Lords is likely to uphold Ravenswood's petition for the restoration of his property (pp. 162–64). Keeping up the pressure, the Marquis has sent Ravenswood the afore-mentioned letter (pp. 99–100), ensuring that Sir William knows of the correspondence. Insecure, the Lord Keeper fears that unless he sides with the Marquis, the nobleman will help Ravenswood to dispossess him. In the absence of Lady Ashton, Sir William forms a plan. By ingratiating himself with Ravenswood and encouraging a marriage between him and Lucy, he will solve all his problems. Ravenswood will not attack his father-in-law, either personally or in court, and the Marquis's position will be weakened. With this in mind, the Lord Keeper has contrived to visit Wolf's Crag, where warmer feelings inconveniently conflict with cold calculation. He is also troubled by the unanswered question: 'what will Lady Ashton say?' (p. 169).

Ch. 16. In the morning, Sir William draws Ravenswood aside to explain the history of the quarrel between himself and Allan, Lord Ravenswood. Ravenswood, regretting his own courtesy, declines to discuss it in the place where his father died. He admits he may have mistaken Sir William's personal character, but makes an impassioned speech in defence of his own rights. Glancing up, he sees Lucy watching him with 'enthusiastic interest and admiration' of his noble features, desolate state and courage (p. 172). Sir William looks on with satisfaction: 'I need fear [...] neither Parliament nor protestation; I have an effectual mode of reconciling myself with this hot-tempered young fellow.' He is in no hurry. 'The hook is fixed; we will not strain the line too soon' (p. 173). He considers neither the pain he may give Ravenswood, nor the harm to his own daughter. At breakfast, Caleb announces that there is a man at the gate waiting to speak to Ravenswood. It is Craigengelt, come on Bucklaw's behalf to challenge Ravenswood to another duel. Ravenswood refuses to take this seriously, insults are traded and Ravenswood threatens to whip Craigengelt. Sir William, who has been watching, divulges that Craigengelt has recently been interrogated by the Privy Council, and is anxious to tell Ravenswood why.

Ch. 17. The Lord Keeper informs Ravenswood that he has been under suspicion of a criminal act, and that if he, Sir William, had not spoken for him, he would by now be in prison or in exile. Seeing Ravenswood's incredulity, Sir William sends Lockhard to fetch his mail box. He gives Ravenswood a selection of papers to read; these reveal the information given to the Privy Council about the 'riot' at Lord Ravenswood's funeral, and prove that Sir William acted as 'an advocate and peacemaker' (see ch. 5 pp. 65–66) in having the case dropped. Ravenswood, filled with gratitude and remorse, takes Sir William's hand and sincerely apologises for distrusting him. A touching reconciliation scene follows and Sir William, genuinely moved, convinces himself that a marriage between Lucy and Ravenswood would be wonderful, until he remembers Ravenswood's poverty – and Lady Ashton. Ravenswood learns that Craigengelt has told the Privy Council 'Some nonsense about your proposing to enter into the service [...] of the Pretender' (p. 182), – an accusation which (although true) was scoffed at by Sir William and the scheming Marquis of A——. Bucklaw's association with Craigengelt is touched upon; Ravenswood sticks up for Bucklaw, saying that he is honourable and Craigengelt a bad influence. He hopes (in vain)

Walter Scott's *The Bride of Lammermoor* 43

that when Bucklaw inherits his aunt's estate, he will seek better company.

Ch. 18. Ravenswood has agreed to spend a couple of days as Sir William's guest. Caleb reacts with horror. Telling Ravenswood that 'it isna for your father's son to be neighbouring wi' the like o' him', he then gives another reason: the prophecy of Thomas the Rhymer which will be fulfilled if he sets foot in Ravenswood Castle. Ordered to elucidate, Caleb falters out the fatal lines (p. 185):

> When the last Laird of Ravenswood to Ravenswood
>   shall ride,
> And woo a dead maiden to be his bride,
> He shall stable his steed in the Kelpie's flow,
> And his name shall be lost for evermoe!

Ravenswood brusquely dismisses this as nonsense and, after the Lord Keeper has generously tipped Caleb with gold (which Caleb tries to give to Ravenswood), he leaves with Lucy and her father. After stopping for lunch at Bittlebrains-House, they arrive at Ravenswood Castle in the afternoon. On the way, Ravenswood has been in cheerful mood, but now gloomier thoughts assail him. He notices all the changes that have been made, especially the removal of his ancestral portraits, replaced by those of Sir William and Lady Ashton and the Lord Keeper's parents: 'And it is to make room for such scarecrows as these, thought Ravenswood, that my ancestors have been torn down from the walls that they erected!' (p. 191). He also notices that in his formal portrait Sir William looks 'henpecked' alongside his wife, who bears in her looks 'all the pride of the House of Douglas' (p. 192). Comparing the hall with the one he remembers, Ravenswood, in a moment touchingly reminiscent of normal boyhood, shows Sir William a corner where he kept his carpentry tools and hunting equipment. Sir William introduces his son Henry, whose impudent blethering is halted when his father tells him to ask the Master of Ravenswood about the hunt. Henry skulks beside his father, whispering, 'I tell you it is the picture of old Malise of Ravenswood, and he is as like it as if he had loupen out of the canvass' (p. 195). Sir William is displeased by this reference to the killing of his predecessor by an earlier Ravenswood (see p. 38), and Ravenswood is displeased to learn that the portrait referred to is now in the room where the maids launder clothes. Only the angelic face of Lucy Ashton restores his good temper.

Ch. 19. On what he intends to be his last day at the castle, Ravenswood and Lucy visit blind Alice. Alice's welcome is less than cordial; after she has touched his face to make sure of his identity (p. 198), she launches into a tirade echoing the anxiety expressed by Caleb, but with greater vehemence: 'but what do you here, Master of Ravenswood? – what do you in your enemy's domain, and in company with his child? [...] Your fathers were implacable, but they were honourable foes, they sought not to ruin their enemies under the mask of hospitality.' This is strong stuff, and Ravenswood haughtily orders her to be silent, assuring her that Lucy has no friend who would 'venture further to save her from injury or insult' (p. 199). Perceiving the truth, Alice responds, 'Then God help you both!' Now Henry appears, making indiscreet remarks about witches which further infuriate Alice. Lucy takes him away, leaving Alice and Ravenswood alone. Ravenswood accuses Alice of unfounded suspicions, but she is unabashed, asking when a Ravenswood ever sought an enemy's house except for revenge, and suggesting that Ravenswood can only have come now 'in fatal anger, or in still more fatal love' (p. 200). She predicts his future, that a marriage alliance will mean accepting the Lord Keeper's bounty, following him into dishonesty and intrigue, thinking and voting as he does and – the killer blow – 'call[ing] your father's murderer your worshipful father-in-law and patron'. She would rather see Ravenswood dead. Accused by Ravenswood of inciting him to blood and revenge, she denies it, but begs him to leave 'these fatal bounds' (p. 201) where he is a danger to himself and to others. Calming down, Ravenswood promises to consider her words. He tries to give her a piece of gold, which she refuses, saying that it is an emblem of Lucy, and once again exhorts him to depart. Ravenswood, knowing her reputation for good sense, asks her seriously where his danger lies. She tells him that Lucy loves him, and warns that, if he remains under Sir William's roof without marrying his daughter, he is a villain, and 'if with the purpose of allying yourself with him, you are an infatuated and predestined fool' (p. 203).

Ch. 20. Back in the forest, Ravenswood weighs up his situation. He credits Sir William's kindness and admits that he loves Lucy, but is still reluctant to marry her. Alerted finally by Alice's solemn words, he decides to leave immediately. His movements veer in keeping with his fluctuating thoughts; shunning the path to the Mermaiden's Fountain, where Lucy is waiting, he takes another path towards the castle. Henry again intrudes, saying that he is going walking with Norman, and that Ravenswood must escort Lucy home. (In the eighteenth century, young women of Lucy's class were not allowed to walk unchaperoned.) Convincing himself that one more meeting can do no harm, Ravenswood turns back. Lucy is seated among the stones where, to a superstitious eye, she 'might have suggested the idea of the murdered Nymph of the Fountain' (p. 205). Ravenswood sees only her beauty and feels his resolution 'melting like wax in the sun'. Yet he steels himself, telling her that they must part. She reacts with grief and bewilderment, assuring him of her father's goodwill, but he replies (suggesting that he is already becoming infected by the notion of predestination) that 'there is a fate on me, and I must go, or I shall add the ruin of others to my own' (p. 206). But he cannot withstand her tears, and soon 'their lips, as well as their hands, had pledged the sincerity of their affection' (p. 207). (Kissing was as far as this tragic couple, frustrated by class, convention and a reticent author, ever came to expressing their sexual passion.)

Ravenswood wants to rush off and tell Sir William, but Lucy wants the engagement kept secret. Clearly she is afraid of her mother, and ashamed of her father's inability to act independently. Ravenswood is offended by the notion that marriage to him could be deemed unsuitable; he tells Lucy bluntly of his former lust for revenge, impressing on her 'the price at which I have bought your love – the right I have to expect your constancy' (p. 208). Lucy too is offended that he should question her fidelity, but their spat ends with Ravenswood apologising on his knees. They seal their secret engagement solemnly by breaking in two the gold piece Alice refused; Lucy attaches her half to a ribbon round her neck, while Ravenswood puts his close to his heart. As they rise to leave, an arrow whistles through the air, striking a raven perched on an oak tree overhead. It falls, splashing blood onto Lucy's skirt. The bowman is the ineffable Henry, who meets Ravenswood's stern warning of ill-luck to follow (p. 210) with his usual mixture of dimness and effrontery. He makes Lucy cry by telling Ravenswood that she has flirted with twenty gentlemen, then makes matters worse by adding: 'what does the Master of Ravenswood care if you had a hundred sweethearts?—so ne'er put your finger in your eye about it' (p. 211). Meanwhile, Sir William has received a letter from a correspondent who is promoting the formation of a new government led by the Marquis of A——. Taking Sir William's reluctance to commit as a tacit agreement, he proposes a visit by the Marquis to Ravenswood Castle to seal the deal. Sir William accepts, delighted to have Ravenswood present and Lady Ashton absent. Ravenswood is pleased to have an excuse to stay.

Ch. 21. During the preparations for the Marquis's visit, Ravenswood observes contemptuously Sir William's interference in every detail; not belonging to 'a family of rank' the Lord Keeper cannot delegate or restrain his need for ostentatious display. 'I am worn out by these miserable minutiae of the buttery, and the larder, and the very hen-coop' (p. 214) Ravenswood tells Lucy – a prelude to other differences (pp. 215–16). Lucy sees Ravenswood's pride and disdain for her upbringing, while he wonders if he can live with a partner so soft and flexible. Lucy repudiates this view of herself: 'though I will never wed man without the consent of my parents, yet neither force nor persuasion shall dispose of my hand till you renounce the right I have given you to it' (p. 217). The lovers' arguments do not, however, affect their loving intimacy, and Sir William is too busy to heed his neighbours' criticism of it, and of the length of Ravenswood's visit. Among the critics is the new Laird of Girnington, aka Bucklaw, and his 'squire and bottle-holder' Craigengelt. Bucklaw's newly acquired wealth (pp. 217–18) has thwarted Craigengelt's attempt to lure him to St Germains but, his hatred of Ravenswood undiminished, Craigengelt still tries to persuade Bucklaw to reissue his demand for a duel. Bucklaw refuses, remembering the occasion when Ravenswood had spared his life but, his eviction from Wolf's Crag still rankling, he is open to persuasion that, with his new prosperity, he might get revenge by stealing Lucy from Ravenswood. In a crude, cynical conversation (pp. 219–26) a plot is designed. Bucklaw remembers that he has a cousin in Northumberland, Lady Blenkensop, whom Lady Ashton is visiting on her way back from London. Since he has legal papers to send to Lady Blenkensop, it is decided that Caigengelt will deliver them, taking the opportunity to mention Bucklaw's proposal and fill Lady Ashton in on what is happening at Ravenswood Castle. Bucklaw gives Craigengelt money to replace his greasy clothing and orders him to bring half a dozen bottles of Lady Girnington's Burgundy.

Ch. 22. Craigengelt, handsomely dressed, arrives at Lady Blenkensop's. Despite surprise at his vulgarity, she and Lady Ashton, wanting a third player at cards, take a charitable view of his faults. Informed of Bucklaw's proposal, Lady Ashton, seeing a suitable marriage for Lucy and advancement for Sholto (Bucklaw, as Laird of Girnington, now has the right to nominate a Member of Parliament), is enthusiastic. Craigengelt first alarms her with hints about what is happening at Ravenswood Castle; more fully informed, she vows to take vengeance on Sir William for flouting her 'matrimonial authority' (p. 229). Next morning, she leaves for home. At Ravenswood Castle Sir William, his wife forgotten, calls Lucy, Henry and Ravenswood to the terrace to watch for the arrival of the Marquis of A——, expected the same day. Two roads, one from the east and one from the west, converge outside the Castle. The Marquis's front-runners appear to westward, followed by a cloud of dust thrown up by his carriage and outriders. Sir William is so excited that he scarcely hears Henry's words: 'There is another coach and six coming down the east road, papa—can they both belong to the Marquis of A——?' (p. 231). The race between the coachmen of the Marquis and Lady Ashton is hugely entertaining – though not to the watchers on the terrace. When it dawns on Sir William who is in the second carriage, he panics, as does Lucy. '"It is my mother—it is my mother!" said Lucy, turning pale as ashes' (p. 232). All three Ashtons withdraw from Ravenswood, who feels slighted, and orders his horse to be saddled for a quick getaway. It seems the two carriages will crash, but Lady Ashton, recognising the Marquis and conscious of his right of precedence, orders her coachman to give way. Sir William greets the Marquis politely, only showing his confusion by introducing Lucy as his wife. A tense encounter between Lady Ashton (escorted by Craigengelt) and the Marquis (p. 236) is followed by a blazing row between husband and wife (p. 237–40). Lady Ashton bawls out Sir William, ordering him, in a reprise of the earlier Bucklaw/Ravenswood incident, to evict Ravenswood because his bed is needed for Craigengelt. When he refuses, she writes an offensive note to Ravenswood and sends it by her maid. Sir William responds weakly, 'I wash my hands of it entirely' (p. 240) and escapes into the garden. He returns to find Ravenswood gone and the Marquis, who has read the note and is outraged at the insult to his kinsman, threatening to follow. Lady Ashton appears, having interviewed Lucy, to inform the Marquis that Ravenswood 'has abused the hospitality of this family, and Sir William Ashton's softness of temper, in order to seduce a young person into engagements without her parents' consent' (p. 241). After much trading of insults, the Marquis recalls his need of Sir William's support, and decides to stay for dinner. Bucklaw and Craigengelt are guests at this extravaganza. Lucy is absent (p. 242–43).

Ch. 23. Having arranged to meet the Marquis at Tod's-hole, either that night or next morning, Ravenswood rides away from his ancestral home, his emotions in turmoil. In confusion, he wanders onto a path leading to the Mermaiden's Fountain. He cannot help remembering the legend, and that much of Alice's prophecy has come true. What happens next, the narrator remarks, 'could not be called a Scottish story, unless it manifested a tinge of Scottish superstition' (p. 245). Approaching the fountain, Ravenswood's horse takes fright, and he sees a figure standing where Lucy had previously sat. Thinking it must be Lucy, he calls to her, but then recognises Alice, grey-shrouded and with silently moving lips. When he moves, she glides backward and disappears. Deeply disturbed, Ravenswood thinks the previously unthinkable, wondering whether he must 'adopt the popular creed, and think that the unhappy being has formed a league with the powers of darkness?' (p. 247). He goes to Alice's cottage, where he finds her dead. Her weeping maidservant tells him that at the onset of her 'mortal agony' Alice sent a peasant to fetch Ravenswood from the castle. When he failed to return, she prayed that she might see her master's son once more, and renew her warning. She died as the village clock chimed one (p. 247). Ravenswood remembers hearing the sound just before he saw Alice in the wood. Sending the girl to summon help, he covers Alice's face and sits down to wait, unable to shrug off superstitious dread. Soon three old women arrive to prepare the body for burial, a task they relish. Their appearance and ghastly smiles remind Ravenswood of the witches in *Macbeth*; he gives them money, and asks where he can find the sexton to arrange the funeral. The answer is near Tod's-hole, where 'there has been mony a blithe birling [carousal]—for death and drink-draining are near neighbours to ane anither' (p. 250). Leaving, Ravenswood hears a ghoulish, croaking conversation in Alice's garden, as one old woman who, distastefully suggesting that she would enjoy laying out Ravenswood's corpse, questions another about his fate. 'It is written on his brow, Annie Winnie,' replies Ailsie Gourlay, 'that hand of woman, or of man either, will never straught [straighten] him—dead-deal will never be laid on his back [...] I hae it frae a sure hand' (p. 251). Ravenswood, riding away to the eerie graveyard, is overwhelmed by superstitious fears.

Ch. 24. After a disturbed night, Ravenswood rises early to find the sexton, absent the previous day, at the deserted graveyard. The old man mistakes him for a 'wedding customer', revealing that as well as gravedigger he is also a fiddler. Ravenswood explains his errand, saying that he wishes Alice to be buried beside her husband. The garrulous sexton remarks that since Alice was a witch, her grave must be six feet deep, 'or her ain witch cummers would soon whirl her out of her shroud' (p. 255). Unaware of the stranger's identity, he rambles from speculation about Ravenswood's relationship to Alice to his own grudge against Allan, Lord Ravenswood, who took him to the battle where he was injured, then demoted him from household trumpeter to gravedigger. He grumbles about his mean housing and loss of respect, and reviles Lord Ravenswood for allowing his affairs to go to the dogs and 'let[ting] in this Sir William Ashton on us, that will gie naething for naething' (p. 259). Reeling from the lack of respect revealed in this tirade, Ravenswood has further to endure gossip about himself and Lucy, and sneering predictions of how Lady Ashton will treat her son-in-law (p. 259–60). Even the arrival of the Marquis does not daunt the insolent sexton, who pursues him with offers of fiddle music.

Ch. 25. On the way to the inn, the Marquis tells Ravenswood that he saw Lucy too briefly to form a certain judgement, but that in his opinion Ravenswood could do better. Ravenswood is displeased, and the following exchange makes clear that the Marquis's only concerns are to get what he wants politically and to avoid the personal shame he would feel should his kinsman form a 'degrading and dubious situation with these Ashtons' (p. 263). Although he admits that Sir William likes Ravenswood, Lady Ashton does not; the Marquis is particularly peeved because Lady Ashton rejected outright his defence of Ravenswood. He says that Ravenswood would get better terms by appeal to the House of Lords than by marrying Lucy. Ravenswood replies that he wishes to marry Lucy, not her parents; he does not care about squeezing money or land out of Sir William, and will only give up Lucy if she herself terminates the engagement (p. 264). While they are at lunch, a message arrives telling the Marquis that his political calculations have been correct, and 'he saw almost within his grasp, the pre-eminence for which he had panted' (p. 265). The atmosphere lightens, and the Marquis, ignoring Ravenswood's anxious attempts to dissuade him, invites himself to spend the night at Wolf's Crag. Ravenswood sends a messenger to warn Caleb – cue another interlude of farce, in which Caleb fakes a fire at Wolf's Crag, which he warns may blow up the tower, since there are thirty barrels of gunpowder in the cellar. He is successful in diverting Ravenswood and the Marquis to Wolf's-hope, where Caleb is restored to favour, being credited with fixing Girder's appointment as Queen's cooper. In fact, it was Lockhard who had told Sir William how Caleb had obtained supplies for his visit to Wolf's Crag, and Sir William who, amused by the story, had recommended Girder for the post (p. 270).

Ch. 26. The Marquis and Ravenswood are received at Wolf's-hope with offers of accommodation for all and the promise of a lavish dinner at the Girders' for the principal guests. Ravenswood goes out, feeling melancholy, to look at his burning tower; he is irritated by the eagerness of some village boys to see their former liege-lord's dwelling 'blaw[n] up in the lift like the peelings of an ingan' (p. 275). He is distracted by Caleb, who tells him not to worry – it was all a trick. He explains how he made a bonfire in the courtyard to simulate a house-fire, and how the cellar had been used some years ago as a secret arsenal for an abortive rebellion in which the Marquis was implicated. Not that there is now any danger – the unused gunpowder was taken off by smugglers, sold by resourceful Caleb for gin and brandy (pp. 275–79). Back at the Girders' cottage, the Marquis and Ravenswood sit down to the promised feast, the Girders too aware of their station in life to sit with them. The Marquis retires to the rarely used best bedroom, which is vividly described (pp. 280–81). Ravenswood occupies the Girders' own bedroom, which (in a nod to the Dick Tinto narrative) is dominated by a portrait of John Girder painted, not entirely successfully, by 'a starving Frenchman'. This references timeless village attitudes: the sitter's aspirations and status as the richest man in the village, and his neighbours' sneering at his presumption (pp. 281–82). After breakfast next morning, amid elaborate farewells and tipping of the servants with money which Girder plans to appropriate later (p. 283), Ravenswood gives Caleb what money he has left and joins the Marquis in his carriage.

Ch. 27. In Edinburgh, political change happens peacefully and the Marquis comes briefly to power. The winners and losers in government are set out, and those named who are prepared to change their loyalty to avoid ruin (pp. 285–86). One perceived way of currying favour with the Marquis is to support the right of Ravenswood to recover his title and lands. This threatens Sir William Ashton (no longer Lord Keeper) to whom Ravenswood writes candidly, asking his permission to marry Lucy and promising to be accommodating in the matter of his claim. He also writes a placating letter to Lady Ashton and a loving one to Lucy. He receives a vicious reply from Lady Ashton, an equivocating one from Sir William, and from Lucy a deeply troubling note saying: 'I am sore beset, but I will be true to my word, while the exercise of my reason is vouchsafed to me' (pp. 288–90). Ravenswood is filled with alarm, but after trying in vain to make contact, is forced to leave Scotland 'upon the important mission which had been confided to him' (p. 290). Extracting from the Marquis a promise not to act against Sir William in his absence, he disappears from the scene (p. 291).

Ch. 28. A year passes, and Ravenswood is still abroad. The changed condition of the Ashtons is discussed at Girnington by Bucklaw and Craigengelt. Bucklaw is in a bad mood; his proposal has been approved by Lucy's parents and her politically ambitious brother, and, as it seems, by Lucy herself, but Bucklaw is still hesitant. He is honourable to the degree that he would not pressurise Lucy; he cannot understand her change of mind and suspects her mother who 'understands every machine for breaking in the human mind' (p. 294). He cannot believe either that Ravenswood has given up the engagement.

It transpires that a 'Captain Westenho', one of Craigengelt's ilk (p. 294) and doubtless in the pay of Lady Ashton, has been spreading a rumour that Ravenswood is to be married to someone else – hence Lucy's apparent acquiescence. Informed by Craigengelt of the Marquis's disparagement of Lucy, 'the pale-cheeked daughter of a broken-down fanatic' (p. 294) and his opinion that 'Bucklaw was welcome to the wearing of Ravenswood's shaughled shoes', Bucklaw flies into a rage, swearing vengeance on Ravenswood and the Marquis (p. 295).

Ch. 29. Next morning Bucklaw and Craigengelt arrive at Ravenswood Castle, where Bucklaw, 'stammering and blushing', requests an interview with Lucy. Lady Ashton agrees, provided that she herself is present. Bucklaw assents, losing the opportunity to find out Lucy's real feelings. Lucy is brought in, outwardly calm, and while Bucklaw havers, fixes her eyes on her embroidery. Lady Ashton prompts her: 'Lucy, my dear [...] have you heard what Bucklaw has been saying?' (p. 297). Lucy has not. With false gentleness, Lady Ashton wheedles her and makes excuses to Bucklaw for her nervousness. Lucy looks around her in 'fear [...] mingled with a still wilder expression' (p. 298) – it is chillingly clear to the reader that her sanity is now compromised. Bucklaw apologises to Lucy for his bluntness, then tells her that as his wife she shall have everything she wants – on condition that his old playfellow 'Craigie' will have a place in the household. Again Lady Ashton answers, assuring him that Lucy cannot object to the 'blunt, honest, good-natured creature, Captain Craigengelt' (p. 298), and reiterating that Lucy will be guided by her parents. Bucklaw eventually manages to request an answer from Lucy's own lips. Her only answer is addressed to her mother: 'I *have* promised to obey you,—but upon one condition' (p. 299). It is revealed that Lucy has twice written to Ravenswood, at her mother's dictation, asking whether he wishes to continue their engagement. Until she receives an answer, she will not budge. Bucklaw, who refers to himself as 'a plain, good-humoured young fellow', behaves well, saying that he wishes Lucy to have time to make up her mind. Lucy is grateful but, as Bucklaw leaves, Lady Ashton gives him the date of St Jude's day when 'we must all be ready to *sign and seal*' (p. 301). This highly charged scene is disrupted by the boisterous arrival of Henry, to demand from Lucy's work-box ribbon to make new garters and silver wire to fasten bells to his hawk's jesses [leg straps]. Lucy sadly compares herself to the hawk's prey, but Henry scampers off 'with the thoughtless gaiety of boyhood', leaving her to reflect on her isolation: 'alone and uncounselled, I must extricate myself or die' (p. 302).

Ch. 30. During Ravenswood's absence, the Marquis of A—— has vigorously promoted his claim in the House of Lords, incurring the outrage of his political opponents, distressing Sir William and infuriating Sholto and Lady Ashton. Even Lucy feels that her father deserved better from Ravenswood (p. 304). She is pressed to break an engagement 'scandalous, shameful and sinful [...] calculated to add bitterness to the distress of her parents' (p. 305). Lucy bears her father's complaining and Sholto's 'taunts and occasional violence' bravely, but her mother's ceaseless persecution wears her down. Ravenswood's and Lucy's letters are intercepted and burnt by Lady Ashton, and the rumour that Ravenswood is 'on the eve of marriage with a foreign lady' (p. 306) is repeated to Lucy, sometimes 'in the tone of malignant pleasantry', sometimes as 'a matter of grave and serious warning' (p. 307). By bribery of her attendants, Lady Ashton ensures that Lucy lives in a 'leaguered fortress', a situation Lucy does not fully understand until Henry spells out that she is now a prisoner in her own home (p. 308). As her vivid imagination fills with evil characters from legend rather than benign ones, Lucy's mental and physical health deteriorates: 'her hectic cheek and wandering eye gave symptoms of what is called a fever upon the spirits'. Lady Ashton shows no motherly compassion, and resorts to an expedient which 'the reader will probably pronounce truly detestable and diabolical' (p. 309).

Ch. 31. Lady Ashton's 'diabolical expedient' is to engage, as a nurse for Lucy, the 'wise woman' Ailsie Gourlay, locally regarded as a witch. The narrator makes clear (pp. 310–11) that witchcraft is delusionary, but accepts that its effect on an overwrought imagination like Lucy's could be catastrophic. Ailsie Gourlay resents Lucy's distaste for her physical appearance, but sets herself to win her patient's confidence. She tells her stories of the supernatural which begin mildly, but soon turn darker and more mysterious; in those relating to the Ravenswoods she exaggerates their deathly significance with 'quivering and livid lip' and 'uplifted skinny fore-finger' (p. 312). They feed Lucy's conviction that 'an evil fate hung over her attachment', especially when they impinge on her own circumstances. Omens and interpretation of dreams form the 'visionary traffic' (p. 313) which finally unhinges Lucy's mind. Eventually Sir William, alarmed by his daughter's deterioration, gets rid of the malign attendant, but 'the arrow was shot, and was rankling barb-deep in the side of the wounded deer' (p. 313) – an image that recalls the terrible suffering of the wounded stag at the hunt described in chapter 9. Lucy's parents renew the pressure on her to accept Bucklaw, and are startled when she accedes, though she still insists on Ravenswood's agreement. With it, she will obey them, since 'When the diamonds are gone, what signifies the casket?' (p. 314). Lady Ashton dictates an ambivalently worded letter to Ravenswood, asking for a final answer, but then – as Lucy suspects – suppresses it. Lady Ashton tries to enlist the support of the clergyman Mr Bide-the-bent, stressing to him the impropriety of Lucy's choice. Bide-the-bent agrees, but, hearing Lucy's doubts about the fate of her letter, is unexpectedly sympathetic. If Lucy writes another letter, identical to the first, he promises that he will ensure its delivery, but adds that if there is no answer, she must accept that Ravenswood has abandoned their contract (p. 316). No answer comes before St Jude's day arrives.

Ch. 32. Bucklaw arrives with Craigengelt at the Castle, to witness the marriage contract. The only other attendees are the Ashton family and the minister. Although only four days are to elapse before the wedding, superficially Lucy appears calm, allowing herself to be dressed splendidly in a white gown and jewels which contrast strangely with her pale face and 'unsettled eye'. When Henry arrives to conduct her to the ceremony, even his self-absorbed prattling and hurtful remarks about Ravenswood (p. 318) fail to move her. Lady Ashton propels her into the hall, where Bide-the-bent prays lengthily (p. 319). Sir William, Sholto and Bucklaw then sign the contract. Fumbling with pen and ink, Lucy has scarcely finished signing when a horse's hoofs are heard outside – and a well-known voice. Lucy shrieks, 'He is come!' (p. 320).

Ch. 33. Ravenswood's appearance, haggard and dishevelled, transfixes the company. All but Sholto and Bucklaw show fear, and Lucy seems turned to stone. Recovering first, Lady Ashton demands the reason for 'this unauthorized intrusion' (p. 322) while Bucklaw and Sholto, true to type, issue challenges to fight. Sir William and Bide-the-bent try to silence them, but Ravenswood does so by drawing his weapons: 'I WILL hear her determination from her own mouth; from her own mouth, alone, and without witnesses' (p. 323). When Bide-the-bent ventures that this is reasonable, Lady Ashton vetoes it. The young men again threaten Ravenswood, who waves them off and puts Sir William out of the room. Finally he faces Lucy, who falters, 'It was my mother' (p. 326). Lady Ashton triumphantly concurs, calling on Bide-the-bent to back her up.

Cornered, the minister reads from his Bible a passage from the book of Leviticus, which at first seems to support Lucy's right to choose, but then fatally allows her father to overrule her (p. 326). Made cruel by pain, Ravenswood reproaches Lucy with his own sacrifices; when Lady Ashton shows him Lucy's signature on the contract, he appeals to Bide-the-bent to say whether Lucy signed without duress. On hearing that she did, Ravenswood lays down his half of the gold coin and sternly demands that Lucy return hers. Lucy tries to undo the ribbon at her neck; Lady Ashton cuts it and throws down Lucy's half, along with a stolen paper on which the lovers had pledged their troth. In an achingly poignant moment of doubt, Ravenswood's indignation wavers: 'And she could wear it thus [...] could wear it in her very bosom—could wear it next to her heart—even when—But complaint avails not' (p. 328). Recovering, he brushes away a tear, throws both gold and paper into the fire, and again addressing Lucy cruelly, leaves the room. On the way out, Lockhard hands him a note from Sholto, challenging him to a duel five days hence. Next Ravenswood meets Craigengelt, who delivers Bucklaw's challenge. Irked beyond endurance by Craigengelt's posturing, Ravenswood throws him down a flight of stone stairs. Slowly he rides past Bucklaw and Sholto, looking them in the eye as he raises his hat to each of them. Then he departs 'with the speed of a demon dismissed by the exorcist' (p. 329).

Ch. 34. Despite Lucy's behaviour, veering between 'a sort of flighty levity' and silent melancholy, all her family have reasons for pressing on with the wedding. Bucklaw, who would have demurred had he known the truth, is kept away from Lucy, whose mental state, on her wedding eve, shows itself in skittishness and childish interest in the preparation of her dress (p. 331). In the morning a huge company, gaily dressed, arrives to follow the wedding party to church. Lucy, now melancholy and wild-eyed, is mounted behind Henry, too full of himself to pay attention to her. Lucy is duly married to Bucklaw by Presbyterian rites. Outside the church, food is distributed to the poor, among them the three 'hags' who complain bitterly about their share, and comment ungenerously on the scene. Egged on by her companions, Ailsie Gourlay chillingly prophesies that a burial will soon follow, and that Lucy's 'winding-sheet is up as high as her throat already' (p. 334) – a prediction that rouses compassion even in her hardened companions. At the castle, a costly feast and much wine are provided, with music and dancing afterwards. Excusing Lucy, Lady Ashton leads off with Bucklaw but, before they can dance, she notices that the portrait of Sir William's father has been replaced by that of fearsome Sir Malise Ravenswood. Recovering from shock, she declares that a servant, a 'crazy wench' (p. 336), has swapped the paintings – an unfortunate phrase, in view of Lucy's condition. In fact, the culprit was Ailsie Gourlay.

Lucy leaves the hall and, an hour later, Bucklaw follows her upstairs. The party continues until interrupted by a shrill, piercing cry. Sholto rushes out, followed by his parents; he has difficulty entering the bridal chamber because something is lying against the door. It is Bucklaw's body, covered with blood. Sir William and his wife search the room, discovering Lucy in a fireplace, 'couched like a hare [...] her nightclothes torn and dabbled with blood [...] her features convulsed into a wild paroxysm of insanity' (p. 337). She says, 'with a sort of grinning exultation, — "So, you have ta'en up your bonny bridegroom?"' (p. 338) [allegedly the words of Janet Dalrymple], and dies the next night without speaking again. Bucklaw recovers, 'a sadder and a wiser man' (p. 339) and, with new dignity, refuses to discuss what happened. He dismisses Craigengelt from his company and goes abroad, never to return to Scotland. To readers who may find the story 'overstrained, romantic and composed by the wild imagination of an author, desirous of gratifying the popular appetite for the horrible' (p. 340), the answer of Scott/Pattieson is that it is 'AN OWER TRUE TALE'.

Ch. 35. Far fewer attend Lucy's funeral than came to her wedding, but the three 'hags' are there to see the bride's coffin carried to the vault, and share in another food distribution. Ailsie Gourlay gives gleeful vent to her resentment against the Ashtons, while the others ply her with questions about the 'supernatural' significance of the events. She draws their attention to a mysterious thirteenth figure among the mourners 'that they ken naething about; and, if auld freets [superstitions] say true, there's ane o' that company that'll no be lang for this world' (p. 342). Accosted by Sholto and accused of murder – a crime which he sadly admits – Ravenswood, the uninvited guest, shrinks from yet more bloodshed. He tries to dissuade Sholto from duelling, pleading with him to enjoy his life and leave Ravenswood to be killed by another. Only when Sholto swears that, if his challenge is refused, he will make 'the very name of Ravenswood [...] the sign of every thing that is dishonourable, as it is already of all that is villainous', does he accept that he, the last of the Ravenswoods, must ensure that 'the name shall be extinguished without infamy'. They agree to meet at 'The links by the sea-shore to the east of Wolf's-hope—the hour, sun-rise—our swords our only weapons' (p. 344). After the funeral is over, Sholto goes to an inn near the shore, to be ready in the morning. Ravenswood returns to Wolf's Crag. Caleb, having heard of Lucy's death, tries to comfort him, but Ravenswood, after drinking too much and refusing food, spurns the old servant's concern; he will spend the night in the room where his father died and 'in which SHE slept on the night when they were at the castle' (p. 345). While Caleb prays and creeps about outside the door, Ravenswood passes the night hours walking the floor and suffering 'paroxysms of uncontrolled agony' (p. 345). When Caleb finds him in the morning selecting the sword most likely to give Sholto the advantage, he knows what is afoot, but all his pleading cannot stop Ravenswood's departure. Leaving the purse of gold thrown to him by Ravenswood on the pavement, Caleb follows him in terror, remembering the prophecy of the Kelpie's Flow (p. 347). He sees his master reach the fatal spot, and suddenly disappear. The impatiently waiting Sholto has the same experience. Only his horse's hoofprints show the fate of 'the Last Laird of Ravenswood'; all that remains of him is one sable feather, floating on the tide. Caleb's life has 'lost its salt and its savour' (p. 348), and he follows his master soon after. Sholto Ashton, dies in another duel, followed quickly by his afflicted father. Henry dies unmarried, and only the implacable, unrepentant Lady Ashton lives into old age.

8: CHARACTERS IN *THE BRIDE OF LAMMERMOOR*

Edgar, Master of Ravenswood
Ravenswood, aged twenty, is a classic romantic hero, dark-eyed, black-haired and with 'features [...] dark, regular and full of majestic, though somewhat sullen, expression' (ch. 5 p. 60). The last representative of the aristocratic family of Ravenswood, he has seen his father stripped of his title for supporting the Jacobite cause, his lands confiscated and sold to a middle-class politician, Sir William Ashton. Forced into extreme poverty, Ravenswood lives at half-ruinous Wolf's Crag without comfort or amenity, served only by his old steward and a maid-of-all-work. After the funeral of Allan, Lord Ravenswood, (ch. 2 pp. 31–35) is disrupted by an agent of Ashton's, the Master (a title given him by courtesy, not right) swears vengeance against his father's usurper – a vow leading to angst when he saves the lives of Ashton and his daughter, and falls in love with the latter (ch. 5 p. 56). Ravenswood's conflicting loyalties and his tortured relationship with the wily Lord Keeper, representative of the 'new men' now in the ascendancy in Scotland, create a key tension in the novel.

The paradox of Ravenswood is that although he represents the feudal past, with its mutual loyalties and responsibilities, he has ideas ahead of his time. He is sceptical of the supernatural elements to which his misfortunes are ascribed by others, and more irritated than grateful for his servant's well-intentioned, although dishonest, efforts to conceal his fallen status. In conversation with Frank Hayston of Bucklaw (ch. 8 pp. 100–01) he voices a disinclination to fight for the present-day Stuarts, and gives an unexpectedly liberal view of society's future. His open-mindedness and decency, sadly, make him an easy prey to Sir William's offer of friendship (ch. 14 pp. 158–60), and too willing to go along with Lucy's naive belief that love can heal old quarrels. His tragedy is that, for all his modern beliefs and ideas, he cannot break free without betraying his father and becoming a traitor to his class. Pride of heredity and lordly contempt for Sir William's inability to run his household in the Ravenswood manner (ch. 21 pp. 214–15) are at odds with his intellectual perception that social change is inevitable, even desirable. Indeed, this key tension between loyalty to the past, and recognition of the new demands of the present and future, runs through all of Scott's work.

Ravenswood's love for Lucy Ashton arises from admiration of her beauty and compassion for her helplessness. He is aware of the obstacles to their intimacy – his awkward position *vis-à-vis* her father, his own poverty, class difference and the implacable hatred of her mother. But in Lucy's presence his resistance crumbles. From the scene at Wolf's Crag (ch. 10 pp. 124–27) where, in a spectacularly Gothic thunderstorm, their cheeks first touch, to the crucial meeting at the sexually symbolic Mermaiden's Fountain (ch. 20 pp. 206–09) where he tries to leave Lucy but ends up engaged, Ravenswood follows his heart.

Despite Ravenswood's scoffing at the supernatural, to the less sophisticated people around him, Caleb Balderstone, blind Alice Gray, the 'wise woman' Ailsie Gourlay and her confederates, he is bound to play out a predetermined role. Not until, under great emotional stress, he sees Alice's ghost by the Mermaiden's Fountain (ch. 23 pp. 245–46) and hears that she died only minutes before, does his reason begin to disintegrate. His meeting with the three old women in the garden and their macabre conversation regarding his fate (ch. 23 pp. 250ff) destabilise him further, and he cannot shake off the terrifying suspicion that their words may be true. The man who laughed at Caleb's tremulous repetition of the old rhyme prophesying his death (ch. 18 p. 185) loses the belief that he controls his own actions. His mind gives way to a sense of doom.

The return of Lady Ashton (ch. 22 p. 231ff) and Ravenswood's absence abroad in the service of the Marquis of A—— set in motion the terrible events that close the tale. By the time the frenzied and careless Ravenswood rides to his duel with Lucy's elder brother (ch. 35 pp. 347–48), his soul has been stripped bare. He has lost his fiancée, his title, his ancestral home and even his proud belief in the mutual respect between his ancestors and their vassals. He has nothing left to live for and, had he not died in the Kelpie's Flow, he would have allowed Sholto Ashton to kill him.

Sir William Ashton
Sir William Ashton, an astute and crafty lawyer and politician, is described in detail by Scott (ch. 2 pp. 27–29). An opportunist content to change his political allegiance when it suits him, he has become a powerful figure in the Scottish government since the accession of William and Mary to the British throne. As Keeper of the Great Seal of Scotland, he has grabbed the chance to buy Ravenswood Castle and the lands confiscated from the Master's father, Allan, Lord Ravenswood. Sir William's animosity towards the Ravenswoods arises from contempt for their Jacobite loyalty and Episcopalian beliefs, and from class envy. He is also angry that they have gone to law (ch. 27 p. 289) to get back their lost property – which they might win. The insecurity underlying his grandeur fuels his enmity; he is first encountered (ch. 3 pp. 36–39) pondering the report of the spy he sent to Lord Ravenswood's funeral, wondering how he can use it to bring the Master to heel.

The fateful incident of the bull's attack on Sir William and his daughter, and their rescue by young Ravenswood (ch. 5 pp. 54–56) alter the balance of their mutual dislike, setting in motion a previously unthinkable train of events. Ravenswood and Lucy Ashton fall in love, and Sir William begins to see a way of binding his youthful antagonist by marriage into his family, so seeing off the threat posed by Ravenswood's claim to the estate. The speech of Sir William on his carefully planned visit to Wolf's Crag (ch. 17 pp. 178–81), in which he suggests burying the hatchet, is crucial to understanding his lawyerly persuasiveness and ability to charm. Not only does it persuade Ravenswood to be reconciled, it makes the reader question whether Sir William is such a bad egg after all.

Scott, the fairest, least judgemental of authors, is scrupulous in giving scheming Sir William a human face. The Lord Keeper is a loving, if manipulative, father, and, although his main concern is always his own interest, he is not blind to Ravenswood's good qualities. His fatal weakness is a domestic one; he is unable to stand up to his domineering, aristocratic wife, whose enmity towards Ravenswood is unrelenting. The return home of the terrifying Lady Ashton (ch. 22 pp. 230ff) fairly spoils Sir William's plans, estranges the lovers and propels a succession of shocking events. In an age of male dominance and paternalism, the Lord Keeper proves humiliatingly incapable of controlling what happens in his own household.

Lucy Ashton
Lucy Ashton seems younger than a modern seventeen-year-old. Born at the end of the seventeenth century, she is sheltered, unsophisticated, poorly educated and powerless to change her own life. Indulged by her wealthy father, loved by her brothers but directed in everything by her cold, dismissive mother, she has no meaningful occupation, and no future but to be married off to a country laird, less for love than for money (ch. 3 pp. 41–42). Superficially, her characteristics are physical beauty and an extreme passivity of nature, economically expressed in the spooky little song she is singing when first encountered (ch. 3 p. 39). Scott remarks that 'Lucy's sentiments seemed chill, because nothing had occurred to interest or awaken them' (ch. 3 p. 42), and, under the placid

surface and despite her conventionally ladylike fainting at moments of alarm, she is stronger and more obstinate than she at first appears. With nothing challenging to do, Lucy lives in an imaginary world of old legends and ballads, absorbing ideas 'of ardent devotion and unalterable affection, chequered as they so often are with strange adventures and supernatural horrors' (ch. 3 p. 40). This dangerous inner life feeds her capacity for passionate but repressed feeling, and to her Ravenswood seems the ideal romantic hero. It also makes her vulnerable to the perverted version of the legends forced upon her by the witchlike Ailsie Gourlay, which play a great part in driving her insane.

The tragedy of Lucy Ashton is that love never makes her happy. Like Ravenswood, she recognises their mutual unsuitability; her lover is her father's sworn enemy, and there are profound political, social and religious differences between them. These are cruelly highlighted in their conversation (ch. 21 pp. 214–16), and Lucy is constantly torn by her infatuation with Ravenswood, terror of her mother (ch. 22 p. 232), and sense of duty to her father. Her conviction – owing everything to romantic legend and nothing to experience – that constancy will triumph shows the obstinacy of pent-up passion. Finally believing that Ravenswood has left her for another woman, her illusory ideal is broken and, driven mad by despair, she agrees to marry earthy, unimaginative Bucklaw. Confronted on her wedding night by the reality of loveless sex, she tries to kill him.

Lady Ashton
Lady Ashton is compared (ch. 2 p. 29) to Shakespeare's Lady Macbeth, a ruthless woman who will stop at nothing to raise her husband politically and socially. Thus she exerts a power denied her by the male hierarchy of the world she lives in. Of higher class than Sir William (she is related to the aristocratic family of Douglas), she is handsome, haughty and of a violent

Walter Scott's *The Bride of Lammermoor* 67

temper, though outwardly religious and ostentatiously hospitable when the situation demands. Impudently but aptly referred to by her chosen son-in-law Bucklaw as 'the Lord Keeper's Lady Keeper' (ch. 21 pp. 223), she despises Sir William while using her power of political influence to promote their joint interest. There is no mutual warmth between them and 'there were times when [Sir William] considered his grandeur as dearly purchased at the expense of domestic thraldom' (ch. 2 p. 30). Ambition alone holds them together. Lady Ashton is away from home while her husband concocts his plan to unite the families of Ashton and Ravenswood, although her unseen presence haunts the narrative. Her return to Ravenswood Castle (ch. 22 pp. 229–43), involving a carriage race with a Marquis and a scene of exquisite horror and embarrassment on arrival, would be comical but for its dire consequences.

Lady Ashton has three children, but her relationship with the youngest, Henry, is unexplored. She thinks poorly of Lucy, deriding her as her 'Lammermoor shepherdess' and blaming her apparent lack of spirit on her father's 'more plebeian blood' (ch. 3 p. 41). The mother's love and ambition are centred on her elder son, Douglas Sholto; it will be his task to 'support the untarnished honour of his maternal house, and elevate and support that of his father' (ch. 3 p. 41). Her determination to marry Lucy to Frank Hayston of Bucklaw arises not only from her hatred of the Ravenswoods but also from Bucklaw's possession, in the political system of the time, of the right to nominate a Member of Parliament. It would enhance Sholto's career prospects to be an MP, and, when Lucy refuses to break her engagement to Ravenswood, this unnatural mother will even employ a reputed witch to enforce her will (ch. 31 pp. 310–13). Lady Ashton scorns belief in supernatural powers, although she is held by the ignorant to possess them (ch. 34 p. 334), but she understands and uses deliberately the power of malign suggestion. When finally her evil actions lead to the death of her daughter and the ruin of her family, she shows no remorse at all.

Colonel Douglas Sholto Ashton
As an on-stage presence, Sholto Ashton plays no prominent part in the development of *The Bride*. At the outset, he is travelling abroad (ch. 2 p. 31) in the usual style of a wealthy young man of the period, but shortly afterwards (ch. 3 p. 41) he is described as a soldier. He is said to love his sister more than military advancement or distinction, but his eagerness for her to marry Bucklaw (ch. 28 p. 293) suggests that a seat in Parliament matters more than her happiness. By this point in the novel he is already a colonel – improbably, since he can only be in his early twenties, with arrogance to match. In the closing chapters he sides with his mother, turning against Lucy and scorning her with 'bitter taunts and occasional violence' (ch. 30 p. 305). But his soldierly notion of honour persists. After the fateful signing of the marriage contract between Bucklaw and Lucy (ch. 32 p. 319), he challenges Ravenswood to a duel, a demand repeated on the threshold of the burial crypt when Ravenswood, uninvited, attends Lucy's funeral (ch. 35 p. 343). Frustrated in his lust for revenge by Ravenswood's death in the quicksand, Sholto Ashton dies abroad in another duel (ch. 35 p. 348).

Henry Ashton
Henry Ashton is the wee brother from hell. Aged fifteen, he behaves like a spoilt eight-year-old. He is said to love Lucy, but his pestering demands for her attention are tactless and self-serving. He has little respect for his father and none for the tutor paid to teach him (ch. 18 pp. 193–94), and his only interest is field sports in the company of his father's forester (ch. 20 p. 205). Initially he is afraid of Ravenswood, because of his resemblance to a portrait of his murderous ancestor, Malise of Ravenswood (ch. 18 p. 195) but familiarity restores

his impertinence. Even in the intimidating presence of blind Alice Gray he chatters inanely but dangerously of witchcraft. It is Henry who kills the ill-omened raven (ch. 20 pp. 209–10), and he who, having reduced Lucy to tears by giving her a willow branch (a symbol of mourning for a lost lover), tells her she is now a prisoner in her own home (ch. 30 pp. 307–08). After thoughtlessly remarking that he prefers Bucklaw to Ravenswood, who 'looked like a Spanish grandee come to cut our throats and trample our bodies underfoot', he barely registers her grief as he witters excitedly about the outfit he is to wear at her wedding, and complains that his father will not give him a sword (ch. 32 p. 318).

Henry is blind to the unfolding drama. Credulous, narcissistic and incapable of sympathy, he represents the shallow, underdeveloped human mind. Kitted out in laced cloak and feathered hat and wearing a sword in defiance of his father's wishes, he rides to church with his doomed sister mounted behind him. Only after her death does he recall that Lucy's hand on his felt 'as wet and cold as sepulchral marble' (ch 34 p. 332).

Frank Hayston of Bucklaw
When first introduced, Bucklaw and his disreputable friend Captain Craigengelt are drinking in the inn at Tod's Den (ch. 6 p. 69), and Bucklaw's fondness for drink is the first thing we learn about him. He is 'short, stout, ruddy-faced and red-haired, with an open, resolute and cheerful eye' (ch. 6 p. 69), the complete opposite of Ravenswood, to whom he is constantly compared. Unimaginative Bucklaw has a good opinion of himself; he is not evil, but he is coarse, weak and opportunistic, chronically short of money and openly desperate for his aunt, Lady Girnington, to die and leave him hers (ch. 6 p. 70). Touchy and resentful of Ravenswood's superior manners, he accepts the shelter of Wolf's Crag when in a tight spot, but takes the huff when, after a protracted stay, he is turfed out

to make room for the Lord Keeper and his daughter (ch. 12 p. 146). Egged on by Craigengelt (ch. 28 pp. 293–95) and too conceited to recognise than he is Lady Ashton's stooge, Bucklaw sees no impediment to marrying Lucy. Blundering into a tragedy beyond his comprehension, he rises to dignity only after his bride attempts to murder him. Telling his friends that he has 'neither story to tell nor injuries to avenge' (ch 34 p. 339), he dismisses Craigengelt, goes abroad and never returns to Scotland.

Captain John Craigengelt
Bucklaw's toadying companion Craigengelt is a corrupt, bombastic soldier of fortune, fantastical in appearance and mercenary at heart. He is a chancer whose 'captaincy' is probably self-assumed, and when introduced is acting treasonably as a secret agent for the Jacobite court-in-exile at St Germains (ch. 6 p. 73). He tries to recruit Bucklaw and Ravenswood to fight for the Stuart cause; when this ploy fails he remains Bucklaw's best mate but becomes the enemy of Ravenswood who, bored by his posturing and blustering talk of duels, regards him as a lowlife pest. Craigengelt stokes Bucklaw's resentment against his exclusion from Wolf's Crag. His acting as proxy in Bucklaw's wooing of Lucy (ch. 22 pp. 227–29) is as much an act of spite against Ravenswood as a stratagem to ensure his position in Bucklaw's household. He ingratiates himself with Lady Ashton, and is present at the fatal signing of the marriage contract (ch. 32 pp. 317ff). His last ignominious appearance (ch. 33 p. 329) is when Ravenswood sees red and throws him down a flight of stairs.

Caleb Balderstone
Often in literary tragedy a comical character is introduced, giving an occasional break from the main theme of unrelenting doom. Caleb Balderstone, once Lord Ravenswood's steward but now demoted to the position of unpaid factotum, fills this

position in *The Bride*. Old, starved and shabby, but desperate to maintain the ancestral dignity and consequence of the Ravenswoods in face of their diminished fortunes, he spends most of his energy devising stratagems to hide the Master's poverty from visitors such as Bucklaw, Sir William Ashton and the Marquis of A——. To this end he shamelessly breaks up the kitchen (ch. 11 pp. 128–29), steals food (ch. 12 p. 146), and fakes a fire at Wolf's Crag (ch. 25 pp. 268ff). Set against the cool efficiency of Sir William's valet Lockhard, Caleb's antics can often be entertaining, but provoking and embarrassing to his master. Perhaps Scott is suggesting that the old order is not unquestionably a good one.

The slapstick sometimes sits uneasily with the tragic main theme, but Caleb is more than a comic turn. He is absurd, yet dignified by his devotion and sense of place. His personal loyalty is a reproach to the bitterness of Mortsheugh and Ailsie Gourlay, and to the surly villagers who, refusing to supply food to their former landlord, are willing to see him starve. Caleb, whose 'ideas, his feelings, whether of pride, or of apprehension, of pleasure or of pain, had all arisen from his close connection with the family which was now extinguished' (ch. 35 p. 348), does not long survive the ghastly event at the Kelpie's Flow. He too represents the passing of old values in the upheaval of social change.

Alice Gray

From ancient times, blindness was an affliction associated with power of inward sight and the gift of prophecy. 'Blind Alice' is a solitary Englishwoman living secluded in the forest some distance from a village. Dignified but aloof despite her extreme poverty, she is a marginalised figure, supposed by the ignorant and superstitious to be a witch. She is friendly with Lucy but, in an uncomfortable interview, arranged by Lucy, with the Lord Keeper (ch. 4 pp. 47ff), she proudly affirms her devotion to the Ravenswoods. Spurning Sir William's offer to improve her situation (p. 51), she warns him that he is in danger from young Ravenswood's hotheadedness and lust for revenge – words that go down like a lead balloon. When subsequently visited by Ravenswood in the company of Lucy, (ch 19 pp. 198ff) she treats him harshly, rebuking him for consorting with his enemies and warning him to back off before he destroys the Ashtons and himself.

Ravenswood's seeing of Alice's ghost at the Mermaiden's Fountain (ch. 23 p. 246) signals the arrival of the three 'hags' and the descent into a nightmare, where Alice's forewarnings are fulfilled and evil suffuses the last chapters of the book. Alice is brave and outspoken, but she remains an ambivalent figure. Whether her foresight is supernatural, or merely an intelligent assessment of the situation, remains an open question.

Ailsie Gourlay
Foremost among the three old women who come to prepare Alice's body for burial (ch. 23 p. 249) Ailsie Gourlay alone is given a surname; the others are 'Annie Winnie' and 'Maggie', usually dismissed as 'the paralytic hag'. They are tacitly compared to Alice, but lack her dignity; they are old, unattractive, superstitious and envious, but Ailsie Gourlay (known as a 'wise woman', a euphemism for a witch) has an extra dimension of wickedness. Whether she actually believes in her own occult powers, or uses the credulity of others to her advantage is immaterial. Her malevolence and ability to scare people are real, and first revealed in a chillingly incantatory exchange with Annie Winnie in Alice's garden, overheard by a horrified Ravenswood (ch. 23 pp. 250–51).

In chapter 31 (pp. 310–11), the author interpolates a revealing account of witchcraft in pre-modern Scotland, reflecting Enlightenment views of the subject. This emphasises the evil and cynicism of Lady Ashton's recruiting of Gourlay as a nurse and 'mediciner' to Lucy, who incurs the enmity of the old woman by shuddering at her decrepit appearance (p. 311). By the time Sir William realises what is happening and dismisses her (p. 313), her cynical embellishments of legends relating to the Ravenswoods have fatally unbalanced Lucy's mind.

The final appearances of the three 'hags' are at Lucy's wedding and at her funeral, where they jostle for a share of the food handed out to the poor (ch. 34 p. 333; ch. 35 p. 341). They girn about the inadequacy of their share and comment ungenerously on the action, like the chorus of a Greek play. At the wedding Gourlay, knowing better than anyone Lucy's state of health, predicts her imminent death (ch. 34 p. 334), but also her own fate. Sir William Ashton, she says bitterly, had promised her 'a bonny red gown', a reference to the fire in which a witch burns.

Johnnie Mortsheugh
The gravedigger engaged by Ravenswood to arrange Alice Gray's burial in the abandoned graveyard of the Hermitage is a peasant with a grudge. Mortsheugh, whose name means 'digger of the dead', is contemptuous of class and devoid of loyalty; a reluctant henchman of Allan, Lord Ravenswood, he was obliged to fight on the Royalist side at the battle of Bothwell Bridge (1679), sustaining a chest injury which ended his tenure as trumpeter at the castle. Unaware of Ravenswood's identity, he gives a trenchant account of his travails (ch. 24 pp. 254–60), castigating Ravenswood's father for mismanaging his affairs and complaining about his demotion and present miserable housing. His fortunes improve when he is appointed bedral (beadle) at Ravenswood Church. His last appearance, dressed in a new black coat and with powdered hair, is at Lucy's wedding. Promotion has gone to his head. Threatening to whip Ailsie Gourlay for talk of witchcraft on church premises, he boasts ludicrously: 'I'm half a minister mysell, now that I'm a bedral in an inhabited parish' (ch. 34 p. 334).

The Girders of Wolf's-hope

The Girder family, husband, wife and wife's mother, inhabit the village built to accommodate Lord Ravenswood's tenants, peasants who worked his land, paid rent in the form of produce and were obliged to follow him to war – an arrangement ended by the attainder of Allan, Lord Ravenswood. Since then Girder (variously called Gilbert or John), a cooper, has flourished, as evidenced by the house visited by Caleb on the evening of a christening (ch. 12 p. 142ff), intent on stealing food for the Master's table. The contrast between the bleak ruin of Wolf's Crag and the comfort and ample provision of the Girders' cottage is a comment on the fall of the mighty and the growing prosperity of the lower class, propelled by the waning of feudalism and the dawning age of meritocracy – a constant theme of *The Bride.*

As the most protracted episode of 'light relief' inserted into a tragic narrative, the tale of the Girders is clearly meant to be funny, their rustic antics contrasted with the refined manners of the aristocracy. But despite the vigorous Scots repartee and the absurdity of the situation, modern readers may find it more distasteful than amusing. Social attitudes have changed, and the coarse, threatening behaviour of Girder towards his wife and mother is no longer the stuff of comedy. More entertaining is Girder's attempt, on hearing that the Lord Keeper is at Wolf's Crag, to persuade Caleb to mention Girder's suitability for the vacant position of Queen's cooper (ch. 13 pp. 151–53). When he is appointed Caleb, innocent of any involvement, hilariously becomes the go-to fixer for everyone at Wolf's-hope greedy for promotion (ch. 25 pp. 270–73).

The Reverend Mr Bide-the-bent

Mr Bide-the-bent, minister of Ravenswood parish, plays a small but important part in the narrative of *The Bride.* His name signifies that he bore the trials of hiding among the

Walter Scott's *The Bride of Lammermoor* 75

grassy hills during the 'killing times', which left him disabled by rheumatism. First encountered at the christening party, where he tries to intervene in the fight between Girder and his mother-in-law, he is the strict Presbyterian minister of Ravenswood church, his parishioners ranging from the Ashton family to the poorest villagers. Bide-the-bent's experience as a Covenanter makes him inimical to Ravenswood, an Episcopalian whose father was among his persecutors. This makes his fair-mindedness remarkable.

Having failed, through the agency of Ailsie Gourlay, to divert Lucy from her determination to marry Ravenswood, Lady Ashton enlists Bide-the-bent to use the Bible to confound her recalcitrant daughter. She has rightly assessed the minister's disapproval of the marriage, but underestimates his integrity. Sharing Lucy's suspicion that her letters to Ravenswood have been intercepted by her mother, he offers to send another on her behalf. But this merciful act is of no avail. At the betrothal ceremony of Lucy and Bucklaw (ch. 33 pp. 321ff), it is Bide-the-bent who, reading from the Old Testament Book of Numbers, kills Lucy's hope of using scripture to save her engagement (ch. 33 p. 326). Bide-the-bent has shown surprising kindness, but his belief in biblical authority is unswerving.

The Marquis of A——

Named once as 'Athole' (ch. 3 p. 37), the character of Ravenswood's kinsman owes much to John Murray, 2nd Marquis of Atholl (1660–1724), a politician known for his ambivalent allegiance – he had supported the accession of William and Mary but opposed the Union, and was intermittently suspected of Jacobitism. He nonetheless achieved high office as Keeper of the Privy Seal of Scotland under Queen Anne, and was appointed a representative Scottish peer in the Westminster House of Lords. His fictional counterpart is a Tory activist, in opposition to the Whig government which includes Sir

William Ashton. Ravenswood's hope of regaining his title and land by appeal to the House of Lords rests on the patronage of the Marquis, a temporary rise in Tory fortunes making this feasible. It is fear of eviction that fires Sir William's otherwise improbable promotion of marriage between Ravenswood and Lucy.

Ruthless but politically astute (ch. 8 p. 97) the Marquis, needing allies in the Privy Council, hopes to entice Sir William to change sides. His prevaricating letter to Ravenswood (pp. 98–99), advising him against travelling to the court-in-exile, is part of this ploy. Although always in the background, he makes little actual appearance in the story until his arrival on what proves a disastrous visit to Ravenswood Castle (ch. 30 pp. 303ff), soon afterwards dispatching Ravenswood to the Continent (ch. 27 pp. 290–91) on an unspecified diplomatic mission. (Scott has been criticised for the clumsiness of this plot-device, used to remove Ravenswood from the action. There is no evidence that Ravenswood might have had diplomatic skills, or that he spoke a foreign language.) Once in power, the Marquis no longer needs Sir William, who loses his position. Thereafter the Marquis ostensibly pursues Ravenswood's interest, but his real motive is to thwart Lady Ashton, whom he loathes, and protect his own name from the taint of an unsuitable marriage (ch. 30 p. 304). Like Lady Ashton, he cares nothing for the young couple, and will unscrupulously use them to his own advantage.

9. CONCLUSION

For twenty-first-century readers approaching a novel written two hundred years ago about events which took place a century earlier, it is inevitable that some details, acceptable then, will now strike a discordant note. Apart from domestic violence as a comic theme, there is the occasional use of words now regarded as offensive or demeaning; for instance, we no longer accept the description of a disabled old woman as a 'paralytic hag', or of anyone as a 'crazy wench'. The adjective 'plebeian' is taboo, regardless of its historical meaning. It is also fair to say that some modern feminists have been irritated by Scott's insistence on Lucy's helplessness and passivity, her need of Ravenswood's masculine strength to protect her, and the seeming suggestion that emotionalism, illogicality, and the final descent into madness are particularly female traits. It can only be countered that these are modern readings: others have drawn attention to Scott's implicit critique of patriarchy. Scott was a man of his time. He wrote, as all writers do, in the first instance for his contemporaries, and his contemporaries wouldn't have batted an eyelid. It may also be remarked that Scott's fictional ideal of the perfect relationship between an upper-class couple owed much to his reading of knightly romances in his youth. In fact, his exploration of love in *The Bride of Lammermoor* is deeper and more intimate than in any of his other novels. It is why, like Shakespeare's *Romeo and Juliet*, the tragic story of Lucy Ashton and Ravenswood still resonates with readers today, and continues to enjoy universal relevance.

 Scott himself described *The Bride of Lammermoor* as 'a dismal tale'. Its tragedy is inexorable, inclusive of both private and public life. It raises questions of free will and personal responsibility, action and passivity, and superstition as a metaphor for fate. Above all, it is a tragedy of heredity. Ravenswood and Lucy have personal flaws of character, but they are also the inheritors of the neuroses and fixations of their parents. Lucy's self-made father is at heart irresolute, as terrified as she is of her mother, a domineering woman of high-born pride and fatally vicious temper. Ravenswood's enlightened instincts are constantly in conflict with his sense of entitlement and inherited grievance. They are fated in the sense that it is hard to imagine a happy ending for people carrying such a burden of familial antagonism.

Because of their parents' high public profiles, Ravenswood and Lucy are also participants in a wider national tragedy. *The Bride* is set in a period of religious and monarchical dissent, loss of valued institutions and symbols of sovereignty at the Union, and a destabilising loosening of feudal loyalties in the Lowlands, where the seats of power in Scotland were situated. The political class, comprising greedy opportunists like Sir William Ashton and unscrupulous aristocrats like the Marquis of A——, take advantage of the instability of the times, betraying even close relations in their lust for power.

The terrible conclusion of the story is that even great love is not strong enough to bear the weight of such a heritage. Lucy, her constancy driven to breaking-point by the pitiless persecution of her own mother, loses her reason, attempts murder and dies. Ravenswood, tormented first by the belief that he has sacrificed his integrity for a worthless passion, then by remorse for his cruel treatment of Lucy at their last meeting, rides to his death in the Kelpie's Flow. Ironically only unimaginative Bucklaw, untroubled by omens, superstition or the notion of fate, survives the maelstrom in which he played such a dramatic part.

10. FURTHER READING

a) **Works by Walter Scott**
   Waverley (1814)
   Guy Mannering (1815)
   The Antiquary (1816)
   Old Mortality (1816)
   Rob Roy (1817)
   The Heart of Midlothian (1818)
   Ivanhoe (1820)
   Redgauntlet (1824)
   Sir Walter Scott: Selected Poems, ed. James Reed (Fyfield Books: Manchester, 1992)

b) **Biographies and Critical Works**
   The Laird of Abbotsford A. N. Wilson (Oxford University Press: Oxford, 1980)
   Scott on Himself ed. David Hewitt (ASLS: Edinburgh, 1981)
   Walter Scott: The Making of the Novelist Jane Millgate (University of Toronto Press: Toronto, 1984)
   Brian Hollingworth, 'The Tragedy of Lucy Ashton, the Bride of Lammermoor', *Studies in Scottish Literature* Vol. 19 (1984)
   The Journal of Sir Walter Scott ed. W. E. K. Anderson (Canongate: Edinburgh, 1988)
   Legitimate Histories: Scott, Gothic, and the Authorities of Fiction Fiona Robertson (Clarendon Press, Oxford 1994)
   The Life of Walter Scott John Sutherland (Blackwell: Oxford, 1995)
   Gerry H. Brookes, 'Freedom and Responsibility in *The Bride of Lammermoor*', *Studies in Scottish Literature* Vol. 31 (1999)

The Edinburgh Companion to Sir Walter Scott ed. Fiona Robertson (Edinburgh University Press, Edinburgh 2012)

Sir Walter Scott: A Life in Story Eileen Dunlop (National Museums of Scotland: Edinburgh 2016)

c) **Online resources**
Abbotsford: Sir Walter Scott's home
www.scottsabbotsford.com

Edinburgh University Library: Walter Scott digital archive
www.walterscott.lib.ed.ac.uk

The National Library of Scotland
www.nls.uk

Project Gutenberg: e books of Scott's works
www.gutenberg.org/ebooks/author/59

Lightning Source UK Ltd.
Milton Keynes UK
UKHW021513030419
340420UK00005B/171/P